EARLY COMMENTS ON THIS BOOK:

The first impression one receives from this book is that Bill Crooks was completely unbelievable and probably "beside himself". Then the thought occurs that this is exactly how people also reacted to Jesus. So the question: "Was Bill deluded, or was he Christlike?" In the end the answer is obvious to the eyes of faith: the sick are healed, the blind receive their sight, and the lame leap for joy. The personal testimonies are undeniable. Here is the fruit of the Spirit in the love, joy, peace and longsuffering that shine through the life of this saintly man. If you would learn of Christ, read prayerfully this story of His servant, Bill Crooks.

John F. Coutts
Chaplain, Royal Canadian Navy (*Retired*)

"Seldom do we meet an individual whose life is infused with such love, power, joy, and effectiveness! This story of Bill Crooks reminds us that God walks among us daily in the gritty reality of our brokeness, suffering, emptiness, and fear; it reminds us, too, that we can be 'healed, restored, forgiven.' Bill tirelessly offered God's grace and gave unsparingly of himself throughout his life. The astonishing accounts of those who knew Bill and were touched by him attest to the truth of the cornerstone of his faith: *ie.* that apart from God our lives are completely unmanageable. Bill challenged all to 'let go', to take this plunge into God's healing, and to follow joyfully God's 'daily marching orders!' The warmth of his penetrating blue eyes and his persistent love come to life in this book. You will be much richer for meeting in these pages this remarkable man."

Dr. Todd Sellick
personal and family counsellor, Winnipeg. Manitoba

"If ever I doubted that the Christian life is possible as an ideal, this book about Bill Crooks dispels that doubt! Here is a person who made 'the Imitation of Christ' a reality. He was truly 'a man for others'. To meet him in these pages is to know him and to be helped by him."

Dr. A. Leonard Griffith
former minister, The City Temple, London, England.

"This is the story of a truly good man, one who was prepared to let his faith commitment lead him to wherever he was needed amd who thereby blessed the lives of countless others with whom he came in contact. The book is 'an inspiring read'."

Dr. Rodney M. Booth
former Executive Producer, United Church Television

"Had I not known Bill Crooks personally, I would have said that the stories told in this book were quite impossible. Bill Crooks was 'one of a kind'. Without doubt, he was the most remarkable man I have ever met. Bill's life was a miracle which produced miracles. I am pleased that his story is now available for everyone to read."

T. G. F.
(a grateful and recovering friend)

"Years ago, like many others, I read *In His Steps* which told about a number of people who ordered their lives on the basis of the question, 'What would Jesus do?' The book was inspiring but, of course, was only fictional. Now, however, *A Man Who Made A Difference* moves us from fancy into fact and shows us what happens when a man really does do whatever Jesus would do. Because it is true, this story is especially challenging. Reading it forces us to question the depth of our own commitment to our Higher Power."

O. C. S.,
(a recovering alcoholic and addict)

A MAN WHO MADE A DIFFERENCE

by the same author:

Published by Evangelical Publishers, Canada,
and by Marshall, Morgan and Scott, Great Britain:

```
ON TOP OF THE WORLD

LET'S FACE IT!
```

A MAN WHO MADE A DIFFERENCE

The True Story of "A Man for Others"

by

Hugh MacDonald

**Trafford Publishing
Victoria, B.C., CANADA**

Copyright © 2000 by Hugh MacDonald

All rights reserved. No part of this book may be reproduced or transmitted in any form or by any means, electronic or mechanical, including photocopying and recording, or by any information storage or retrieval system, without written permission from the author.

Printed in Victoria, Canada

Canadian Cataloguing in Publication Data
MacDonald, Hugh Robert, 1934-
A man who made a difference

ISBN 1-55212-433-9

1. Crooks, Bill, 1924-1997. 2. Alcoholism counselors--Canada--Biography. 3. Drug abuse counselors--Canada--Biography. I. Title.
HV5032.C76M32 2000   362.29'186'092   C00-910865-3

TRAFFORD

This book was published *on-demand* in cooperation with Trafford Publishing.
On-demand publishing is a unique process and service of making a book available for retail sale to the public taking advantage of on-demand manufacturing and Internet marketing.
On-demand publishing includes promotions, retail sales, manufacturing, order fulfilment, accounting and collecting royalties on behalf of the author.

Suite 6E, 2333 Government St., Victoria, B.C. V8T 4P4, CANADA
Phone   250-383-6864   Toll-free   1-888-232-4444 (Canada & US)
Fax   250-383-6804   E-mail   sales@trafford.com
Web site   www.trafford.com   TRAFFORD PUBLISHING IS A DIVISION OF TRAFFORD HOLDINGS LTD.
Trafford Catalogue #00-0098   www.trafford.com/robots/00-0098.html

10   9   8   7   6   5   4

in gratitude

to June,

the other friend who
"came in"
when the rest of my world
"went out"

Alcoholics Anonymous
Acknowledgement and Disclaimer

On page 43 of this book, a passage is quoted from the book, *Alcoholics Anonymous*, Third Edition, Alcoholics Anonymous World Services, Inc., New York City, 1976, page 164

Please note that this excerpt from Alcoholics Anonymous, and Steps One, Three, Eleven, and Twelve of the Twelve Steps, are reprinted with the kind permission of Alcoholics Anonymous World Services, Inc. (A.A.W.S.)

Permission to reprint the Steps along with the excerpt from Alcoholics Anonymous does not mean that A.A.W.S. has reviewed or approved the contents of this book or that A.A.W.S. necessarily agrees with the views expressed herein.

A.A. is a program of recovery from alcoholism only: use of the Steps and the excerpt in connection with programs and activities which are patterned after A.A. but which address other problems (or in any other non-A.A. context) does not imply otherwise.

Please also note that Alcoholics Anonymous has ensured that Bill Crooks' immediate family has given permission for his A.A. membership to be disclosed in this biography.

Contents

Introduction

1. "A Man's Man"   7
2. The Surrender   32
3. In the Service of Love   55
4. The Turning Point   90
5. Wounded to Serve   104
6. Healing Shattered Lives   129
7. A Most Christlike Man   163
8. "He Made Us Know . . ."   187

A Final Word   204

INTRODUCTION

The American evangelist, Dwight Moody, sometimes used a dramatic sentence in his sermons: "The world has yet to see what would happen if a man were to give himself completely to the service of Jesus Christ!" No doubt, these words were intended to stir his hearers to make their own commitments to Christ; but, in fact, Moody was overstating his case. Had he been more concerned for accuracy, he should rather have said, "The world has *only rarely* seen what happens when men and women give themselves completely to the service of Jesus Christ!" Total commitment to Christ may be rare, but it is certainly not unknown. As we look back across twenty centuries, we see people who are remembered because beyond question they did give their all to the God who had revealed Himself to them in Jesus. Names such as Dietrich Bonhoeffer, Albert Schweitzer, Father Damien, William Carey, and a thousand others still shine through history as examples of devotion and service to Christ.

2

Not all saints[1] earn a place in history or make their way into the headlines; there are many others who, having humbly witnessed for their Lord and having served Him in their own ways, have been content to fade into obscurity. Often, only after their lives are over do those who knew these people come fully to appreciate how remarkable they were. For they are remarkable, these hidden saints among us!

Moody may have overstated his case. Essentially, however, he was right: absolute commitment to the "Highest" is very rare. Almost all of us who claim some level of spirituality or religious dedication draw back from the full implications of our creed, whatever that creed may be. As some would-be disciples said to Jesus so long ago, we too find ourselves saying, "Lord, I will follow you; but first I must do this." Occasionally, however, if we are very fortunate, we do come upon a person whose commitment to his Lord has no boundaries and who fully lives out his faith. Such a person seems to incarnate God's love, forgiveness, and compassion. Christians would say that such a person embodies Christ. Such a person was Bill Crooks.

---

[1] A reader should note, perhaps, that the word, "saint", does not refer to someone who is "perfect" but rather to someone who is dedicated: "saintly", "holy", and "dedicated" are virtual synonyms.

This book about Bill incorporates the contributions of many people. They have shared in its writing because they want to express their admiration for Bill and their gratitude for the impact he had upon their lives. They have shared in this project, too, because they want others to come to know Bill. At the beginning of this Twenty-First Century, there are many critics who imagine that the spiritual life is unrealistic and impossible and who say that Christianity simply "doesn't work": those of us who knew Bill believe that his story proves otherwise. Bill was a saint -- not a perfect man and certainly not a pious man -- but a completely dedicated man. Unlike those saints in stained glass windows, Bill wore no halo, but the "Sonlight" of God's love streamed through him. He was very much a "man's man" -- strong, handsome, energetic, brave; but, while retaining all these attributes, he also became "God's gentleman", gentle, caring, giving, serving.

We don't know where you may be as you read this book; perhaps in your own home; perhaps in the waiting room of a doctor's office; perhaps in a chemical dependency unit; perhaps in a hospice. At this moment, your life may be "riding high" without problems or concerns; or you may have reached a place of discouragement with yourself where you are seeking for something or someone who will change your life; or still again events may have dealt you so savage a blow of failure, bereavement, or illness that you are now crushed with despair. Whoever you are, wherever you are, whatever your circumstances, we believe that Bill's story has something to say to you. As you read the pages that follow, it may be that you will find that the Higher Power that changed Bill and that made him the man he was is speaking to you about a great change that can happen in your life, too.

Before we begin Bill's story, there are three difficulties which should be acknowledged. The first of these is Bill, himself. Bill would probably be embarrassed to know that this book has been written -- (although in the end he would agree to it "if it will help others.") When Bill was self-conscious at being praised for something he had done, he would say indignantly, "For Pete's sake! Knock it off!" That voice (and those words) have been heard more than a few times as we have put our stories together. When Bill was used by God to help others, he preferred that no one should know; certainly, he never took credit for the miracles that happened through him. Many of the stories you will read in this book are being told for the first time; they have only come to light as we have contacted people whom we had heard that Bill had helped.

For some readers, a second difficulty may lie in the Christian terminology which is used in much of this book; we hope that this will not be a "stumbling-block" for you. We recognize that the Church and, indeed, all forms of institutionalised religion are increasingly offensive to some people; religious terms often connote dogmas and disputes, rules and regulations, commandments and condemnation -- the very antithesis of the unconditional love which Bill, himself, exemplified. Alcoholics Anonymous in its wisdom has sought to avoid these negatives by referring only to "God as we understand Him" or to "a Power greater than ourselves". Bill was a profound Christian; but, when he was with people who were uncomfortable with traditional definitions of God, he would easily and naturally switch to terminology and concepts which were acceptable. Bill was not interested in converting people to Christian doctrines; rather, his goal was to introduce them to a new way of life. Whoever or whatever "God" is to you, Bill would not argue with you. Please, therefore, don't put this book down because Bill found in Jesus his "Higher Power". However you conceive of God, Bill's story can still speak to you.

There is a third difficulty. Throughout this book, people will be sharing their stories with us and telling how Bill was used by God to inspire, help, and heal them. Often, doing so has involved considerable determination and courage: to speak to us of their former circumstances and to tell of what Bill did for them has sometimes meant that they have had to reopen old wounds and to write of things which they find painful or even shameful to remember. Some of their stories are very personal. We thank them for their honesty. In these pages, as people tell us about Bill, we are following the A.A. principle of anonymity In some instances where total anonymity has been requested, we have modified the story just to the degree that recognition will not be possible: the essence of each story has always remained untouched. Names which appear in quotation marks are pseudonyms; the persons, nevertheless, are very real.

Now, with all that said, let us introduce you to a man who made a difference, a man who was used by his "Higher Power" to enrich and change our lives, a man who in many cases literally saved us from self-destruction (and who sometimes did so at a cost far greater to himself than we realized at the time.) Here is Bill.

CHAPTER ONE

"A MAN'S MAN"

In view of what has been said about Bill in the introduction, this chapter may be surprising to a reader. The first thirty-eight years of Bill's life hold no indication that God would someday use him as a great "life-changer". To the contrary, the first half of his life reads much like that of many other men of his generation. Still, we cannot skip over these earlier years: if we are to appreciate the man that Bill became, we need first to see the man he was.

Bill was born on September 4th, 1924, in Port Arthur. Ontario, Canada, a small city on the north shore of Lake Superior[2]. He was the third of five children born to Herbert and Dorothy Crooks. The Crooks name was and is well-known across Northwestern Ontario. In 1900, Bill's grandfather,

---

[2] Fort William, a sister city of exactly the same size, adjoined Port Arthur. Despite fierce rivalry, the two cities were known as the Canadian "Lakehead"; in 1970, they were united as the new City of Thunder Bay.

James W. Crooks, a pharmacist, had moved from Duluth to Port Arthur (then known as Prince Arthur's Landing) to establish the J. W. Crooks and Company Drug Store. The business had prospered and, within a few years, two other Crooks Pharmacies had opened in the Lakehead. James W. Crooks was also a public servant and city politician; for a number of years, he was a Chairman of the Port Arthur Board of Education and then, in 1921, was elected mayor of the growing city. After James W. died, his son, Herbert, Bill's father, also a pharmacist, had carried on the business. The Crooks Drug Stores continued to prosper and became the largest pharmaceutical chain in Port Arthur and Fort William. The words, "drug store", became synonymous in most people's minds with the name, "Crooks". Bill, therefore, was born into a secure and much-respected family in the Lakehead.

With an older brother and sister, Jamie and Anna Margaret, and two younger brothers, George and John, Bill enjoyed a happy and healthy childhood. Within the home, the defining influence on the family's life was the mother, Dorothy. Herbert Crooks was an Anglican, but Dorothy was a Presbyterian; and it was to St. Paul's Presbyterian Church, a large red-brick church which still stands in the city centre, that Dorothy took the children. (In 1925, the congregation of St. Paul's voted to join Presbyterians, Methodists, and

Congregationalists in the new United Church of Canada; and so Bill, within a year of his birth, had become part of St. Paul's United Church.) While the Crooks household was not noted for intense piety or devotion, Dorothy ensured that her family had a sound moral and religious foundation. For the five children and herself, attendance at worship services and Sunday School was an unquestioned family routine. As a boy, Bill, therefore, was given the fundamentals of Christianity and in due course was confirmed into the full membership of the Church.

As Bill went through adolescence, he was a popular young man with many friends. He had a quiet, gentle manner; but beneath that surface, there was a boyish humour which often erupted in funny escapades and practical jokes. In high school, he was a capable student, but he showed no great interest in things academic. As an athlete, however, Bill excelled! He was noted for his prowess in football, hockey, swimming, downhill and cross-country skiing, and track and field. (This love of all sports remained with Bill throughout his life; up until a few months before his death, he continued to sail, cycle, and play tennis.)

* * * * * * *

With World War II, Bill's life dramatically changed. In 1941, his older brother,

Jamie, enlisted in the Royal Canadian Navy: (Jamie was to become a lieutenant, serving from 1942 to 1945 in the Atlantic and the Mediterranean aboard the corvette, *H.M.C.S Camrose.*) Bill, eager for adventure and moved by the patriotic fervour that was gripping Canada, fretted that he was too young to volunteer. Within a few months, the waiting proved too much for him: although he was only 17 and still only in Grade 11, he "fudged" a few facts and was accepted into the Royal Canadian Air Force. (Dorothy and Herbert were dismayed and considered exerting their parental right to block Bill's enlistment; in the end, however, knowing that Bill's heart was set on following Jamie's example, they let their second son go off to war.)

Thus, while Bill was only in his 'teens, he was given his basic training, taught the skills required by a wireless air gunner, assigned to a bomber crew, and shipped overseas. (Of the seven members of Bill's bomber crew, three came from Thunder Bay and another two from Northwestern Ontario. Bill had known two of his crew mates, the pilot, Don Hagar, and the navigator, Albert Kelly, before they were assigned to fly together. At the time, R.C.A.F. policy discouraged having several members of an air crew all coming from the same small community; if their 'plane were lost, there would be mass grief. Yet, an exception was made for these very young men from the Canadian Lakehead. Because of their youth, they became known as the "Cradle Crew".)

The "Cradle Crew" received their final training on Wellingtons, then were assigned to a Halifax and then finally were entrusted with their own Lancaster[3] which they dubbed the *Solid Sender*. In the two years that followed, the young airmen were to take their *Solid Sender* on a full tour of duty -- thirty-three bombing missions across Germany. (Many of these missions were highly hazardous daylight raids over the Ruhr Valley. The Ruhr was the industrial heartland of Hitler's war machine and, therefore, was the most highly defended part of Germany. The lumbering Lancasters, carrying their heavy bomb loads were easy targets for enemy fire. There were many losses in Bill's squadron; and although *Solid Sender* always made it back to base, more than once it returned with heavy flak damage.)

When Bill returned home after the War, a veteran at 21, he spoke little of his overseas experiences. That they had been harrowing is no doubt. He had watched a number of his friends go

---

[3] The Lancaster was designed to be a heavy night bomber which carried a crew of seven: a pilot, co-pilot, navigator, bombardier, navigator, wireless gunner, nose gunner, and tail gunner. Bill's role as the wireless air gunner made him responsible for radio communications and for manning the top turret with its twin .303 trainable machine guns. The Lancaster normally carried 6 tons of bombs, but could be modified to carry 11 tons on special missions.

down in flames. The Ruhr was a hornet's nest of anti-aircraft guns and fighter defences; by night or day, Allied bombers in that area found themselves swarmed by Messerschmitts and buffeted by German ack-ack. (On one of Bill's missions, the flight panel in the cockpit was damaged; several instruments including the altimeter failed. Without navigational aids, the crew simply followed the rest of the squadron back to base in England. On arrival, however, they found that their flying field was blanketed in fog. With their fuel almost gone, they had no alternative but to attempt a landing. They came down through the clouds, expecting to have several hundred feet of altitude; instead, they found themselves only fifty feet above the ground, hurtling at 150 mph towards a large hangar, straight ahead. Pulling upward with full throttle, Hagar skimmed over the hangar; however, as the 'plane flashed across the building, a rumbling sound was heard. Later, some of the crew climbed to the top of the hangar and found *Solid Sender's* tread marks running across the roof: they had been literally an inch from death!

The risk involved in flying these bombing raids was enormous. Out of every three Canadian bomber crews that undertook a tour of duty, only two survived; (in the Second World War, only submarine crews had a higher rate of casualties.) Today, even on safe, modern, commercial jets, many of us are "white-knuckle flyers" who feel comfortable only when our feet are back on the ground. We can wonder how young men in their 'teens and early twenties climbed aboard their 'planes, once or twice a week, knowing each time that it was highly possible they would never return to base. Death in battle is always gruesome, but to be trapped in a burning aircraft as it plunges to the ground is especially so. Bill's crew witnessed many of these horrors. On one of their daylight missions, a Lancaster beside them in their formation was hit by anti-aircraft fire; there was an explosion and then, in the moments that followed, the entire right wing separated from the fuselage and drifted upwards, beyond their vision. The doomed 'plane continued its momentum for a few seconds and then began a slow tumble, end over end, to its fiery death half a mile below. Bill and his buddies knew the members of that crew; they had had breakfast with them that very morning. What happens to young men who are forced to experience such dangers and horrors week after week?

There were escapes. When possible, air crews were given leaves, allowing them to get away for a week or more from the stress they were experiencing. (On several of his extended leaves, Bill travelled to Scotland where a Highland family "adopted" him and provided him with a "home away from home"; Bill never forgot their kindnesses and continued to write them for many years after the war.). Occasional leaves, recreational activities on the air base, chaplains' messages on Sunday mornings -- these were helpful, but to many men they were not enough. Years later, Bill confided to friends that it was at this point in his life that he began to use alcohol as a way of dealing with stress. A drink or two before climbing aboard would calm his nerves; another two or three after he returned to base would help him forget what he had experienced. Not that Bill became a drunk! Like many other service men, he simply began to discover alcohol as a means of coping with life's tensions.

Bill's tour of duty ended in January, 1945. He immediately volunteered for a second tour, but by then Allied troops were advancing across Germany; mass bombing raids were no longer needed. The crew of *Solid Sender* was disbanded. Bill was assigned to other duties for the remainder of the war. He had made it safely through.

* * * * * * *

Following the war, Bill returned home; but, after all he had experienced, returning to high school was out of the question for him. His younger brother, George was then beginning his studies to become a pharmacist, preparing to enter the family business. John, the youngest of the family, was in high school, eventually to study for a career in dentistry. Jamie, now out of the Navy, was entering the University of Toronto, planning to become an engineer. (Two years later, when Herbert Crooks died, Jamie returned to Port Arthur to help his mother settle the estate; by then, he was beginning to question his choice of engineering as a profession. He met and married Mabel MacNeill; and when he later moved back to Toronto to resume his studies, he took with him not only Mabel, but their newborn son, and with them his decision to switch from engineering to pharmacy. Thus, a few years later, both Jamie and George were partners and pharmacists in J. W. Crooks and Company.)

While his brothers were choosing professional careers in engineering, dentistry, and pharmacy, Bill was taking a very different route. For some time after the war, he worked as a switchman for the Canadian National Railways, a demanding job that involved shift work, much of it outdoors in a climate in which winter temperatures of 30 and 40 below are not unusual. Albert Kelly, the former navigator of *Solid Sender* , was working at the Provincial Paper Mill in Port Arthur; in time, he persuaded Bill to leave the railway and to become a lab technician at the mill. Meanwhile, however, J. W. Crooks and Company was steadily growing in the Lakehead. Eventually, Jamie and George realized that they needed someone to manage the business and to train personnel. Bill was eminently suited for such a position; moreover, through the family estate, he was already a shareholder in the business. In 1952, he left the paper mill to become the buyer and manager for J. W. Crooks and Company. With his acknowledged gifts for working with people, he also became the informal "personnel trainer" for the company.

* * * * * * *

But now we must stop for a moment and return to 1945. As the tens of thousands of Canadian servicemen returned home, there sprang up everywhere special programs and organizations to help them make the transition to civilian life. These groups also assisted young women in dealing with the pleasant but dramatic change of once again having men in their lives. In the Lakehead, the largest and most popular of all these young adult organizations was the "Good Companions" which met weekly in St. Andrew's Presbyterian Church in Fort William. Though Presbyterian-based, it attracted people from all denominations; and though centred in Fort William, its membership spanned, not only that city, but Port Arthur as well. Eventually, more than one hundred "Good Companions" were meeting each week for study, fellowship, and courtship at St. Andrew's. Bill became a Good Companion in 1946; at the first meeting he attended, he met Marion.

Marion Olver was two years Bill's senior, a beautiful young woman, attractive both physically and spiritually. Everyone who remembers her still speaks of her warm personality and her sunny smile. Though gentle and soft-spoken, she was filled with a genuine *joie-de-vivre* that was charming and infectious. She radiated cheerfulness, kindness, friendliness. She was an exceptional athlete; at high school, she had won high honours in many sports. Now, with school behind her, she was working in a bank. Although Marion had been raised within a United Church home, the "Good Companions" of St. Andrew's had pulled her into the Presbyterian fold. Thus, when Bill went to the "Good Companions", Marion was there already. Not surprisingly, she had several suitors; but Bill was not to be deterred. He "recognized a good thing when he saw it": his courtship was brief, determined, and effective. Within a few months, the two were engaged; they were married in St. Andrew's on May 21st, 1947.

The newly-weds established their home in Port Arthur and in the Crooks tradition chose St. Paul's United as their church. Soon, they had made a place for themselves within that congregation, she through her participation in Christian Education work and the women's association, he through positions on various committees and boards. They were faithful in their attendance at worship and generous in their support of the church budget. They came to be regarded as "solid members", the sort of people who after the war formed the backbone of most congregations, people who were in sympathy with the moral values and social concerns of Christianity, people who saw religion as a valid and worthy part of life even if it did not have particularly deep significance for their own lives.

Marion had intended to continue in banking after the marriage, but unexpected health problems began to appear. She had difficulty with her feet; she sometimes stumbled while walking; there were spills on the ski slopes. She would occasionally be overtaken by a strange stiffness in her muscles, a stiffness which brought with it a lack of co-ordination. Doctors confessed that they were puzzled; some suggested that the condition might be a rare variant of multiple sclerosis; others thought that it was an unusual manifestation of muscular dystrophy. When Marion became a mother-to-be in 1949, the pregnancy combined with the illness forced her off her feet and into bed for many months. With the safe arrival of Peter, her condition improved; for a time, she was able to return to such activities as skiing and swimming. The illness never entirely left her, however; to the contrary, as time went by, it became apparent that it was relentlessly progressing. Marion was to bear two more children, a second son, Paul, early in 1953, and a daughter, Carol, at the end of that same year. Again, both turned out to be difficult pregnancies which forced total bed rest upon her. And again, although there was a brief improvement after the births, her physical deterioration steadily continued.

Meanwhile, as we have noted, during these years Bill had moved from the railroad to the mill and from the mill to the pharmacy. He and Marion had bought a comfortable bungalow in one of the better areas of Port Arthur. They were devoted to their children and to each other. By all appearances, they were a happy young couple who, despite Marion's illness, seemed to be well on their way to fulfilling the traditional dream of enjoying a successful marriage, raising three healthy children, surrounding themselves with a multitude of friends, and doing all the usual things to guarantee themselves security and satisfaction. Bridge was a source of enjoyment; so were skiing and swimming; especially so was a beautiful summer cottage on an island in Hawkeye Lake, only an hour's drive from Port Arthur. And, of course, there were the activities at St. Paul's and opportunities for service in the community at large; Bill, for example, was for a number of years a board member and then the chairman of the Port Arthur 'Y'. Everyone admired Bill and Marion Crooks; everyone assumed that they would lead the happy, prosperous lives for which they seemed destined. No one could have dreamed what lay before them.

****

People sometimes ask what Bill was like in these years before the great "change" came over his life. What sort of man was he? His family and friends tell us that, even before 1963, he had certain outstanding traits, traits that were later to be shaped and honed but which always remained central to his character. One of these was his willingness to get involved in any situation where help was needed.

"Three of us went off for a week of duck-hunting in Manitoba; as we headed westward, we came upon a single-vehicle accident. The car, itself, had not been badly damaged; the passengers, both of them women, had managed to get out of the vehicle. They were sitting beside the road, dazed, both with serious injuries. One of them was bleeding profusely.

"The logical and easiest course of action would have been for us to call for an ambulance and then be on our way. Bill, however, would have none of this. We placed the lady who was haemorrhaging across the back seat; Bill climbed in beside her and tried to get her bleeding stopped while her companion climbed into the front seat beside us. We set out,

full speed, for Dryden and the nearest hospital, one hour away.

"The ride was traumatic for all of us, but for Bill it was a special ordeal. An artery had been severed and blood was spurting everywhere, all over Bill, all over the back seat. He had to calm the hysterical woman and bring her bleeding under control. We made it to Dryden, but only in the nick of time: a few more minutes would have been too late. Bill's rapid reaction had saved the woman's life.

"Bill said nothing more about it. We resumed our journey to Manitoba and had a great week of hunting. On our return the following weekend, Bill suggested that we stop in Dryden to see how his 'patient' was doing. He was happy to learn that she had made a full recovery and had already been discharged. He dismissed the incident from his mind and, so far as I know, mentioned it to no one. He was genuinely astonished when, a month later, a beautiful bouquet of flowers arrived at his house; only then did he learn the name of the lady whose life he had saved."

That was certainly Bill! Bill would never stand on the sidelines weighing the odds, waiting for someone else to take action; instead, regardless of the consequences, he would wade in with a reckless courage. Bill, moreover, was always prepared to stand up for the underdog; he refused ever to be cowed by threats or bullying. Sometimes this readiness to act resulted in scenarios which are hard to imagine for those of us who knew only the Bill of later years.

When the situation seemed to demand it, Bill was not adverse to using his fists . . .

"Bill was the sort of fellow you would want on your side if ever there was a rumble; you'd certainly want him to be 'for you' rather than 'against you'. He was strong, fearless, aggressive but he was also a kind and good man. Even if he had been drinking, he would do only what he thought was right. He was always a man of moral principles, but he was not afraid to fight.

"One night, on a street car, on our way home from a late shift at the mill, up at the front of the car we saw a great big guy abusing a man half his size. The rest of us just sat there and listened, but not Bill. Bill walked to the front and said to the man, 'Knock it off!' The bully stood up, and only then did we realize how big he really was! He towered above Bill.

'Who's going to make me?' 'I am,' said Crooks and asked the conductor to stop the car.

"The street car stopped on a deserted stretch of track, and the two men got off. By then the rest of us were willing to get involved, but Bill would have none of it! This was to be a fair fight, one-on-one, (even though Bill was only a middleweight, up against a very heavy heavyweight.) It was a real fight, too. A lot of big punches were thrown; each man went down a couple of times. Finally, the bully threw in the sponge and walked off down the tracks. We got Bill back aboard the street car. In the light, we could see that his right ear had been nearly torn off. We had to persuade him to get stitched up in emergency before he went home."

In some circles, Bill became known as a man who was not afraid to fight whenever he was challenged. This reputation, when combined with Bill's good looks and the fact that he came from a prominent Lakehead family, occasionally led other men (usually while drunk) to try to provoke a fight with him. In such situations, rather like John Wayne in *The Quiet Man*, Bill would brush aside the challenges; however, if a provocateur really persisted, Bill eventually would oblige him.

"One evening, Bill and Marion, my wife and I, and two other couples were sitting around a table in the Flamingo Club. We all had had a couple of drinks and, I guess, our conversation was bit on the noisy side. A drunk came down from the other end of the room; he sought to show his disapproval by standing near our table and sneering at us. We ignored him as best we could; that seemed to anger him all the more.

"Then he spotted Bill. 'Hey, you,' he said, 'I know you. You're Bill Crooks; I've heard that you're the big shot.' Bill stood and suggested that the man go away. The man persisted, 'Yeah, you're the big shot; you think you own the Lakehead.' Again, Bill suggested that the man go away. 'Yeah, I know all about you and your --' As I recall, the sentence was never finished. There was a left to the stomach and a right to the jaw. The intruder crumpled to the floor. Bill walked back and joined us, quite unflustered by the episode. That's just the way Bill was."

Bill's refusal to run away from difficult situations and his readiness to meet whatever challenges were laid before him were reflections of his general response to life: his nature was always to take risks, to gamble on outcomes, to live for the instant and not to worry about what lay ahead. He, for example, was an excellent skier who knew exactly what he was doing on the slopes; but nothing delighted him more than to schuss a dangerous hill, simply to prove to himself that he could do it. There were, of course, spills and accidents; the worst of these occurred one day when Bill was on the highest run in Vail, Colorado.

"Bill and Marion, and my wife and I had long been planning a trip to California with a stop en route at Vail, Colorado. This was a long-held dream, especially for Bill. We all knew that Bill needed a break; his work in the family business was quite heavy, and in addition he had been carrying the extra burden of heading up the fund-raising drive to build a new swimming pool at the 'Y'. We planned to spend a few days skiing at Vail and then to move on to California.

"Bill was an all-out skier, always choosing the most challenging slopes and taking them at high speed. The first couple of days at Vail, Bill and I had skied with our wives down all the standard slopes. We all had done some pretty exhausting skiing. Bill wanted more, however, and so he persuaded me to join him in a day of skiing 'the highlands' at Vail.

"Our final run was from 10,000 feet. Halfway down, something went wrong for Bill on one of the moguls. He was ahead of me, and I saw him fall. As I flashed by, he yelled that he needed help! I could see right away that he surely did! He had suffered a radical fracture of his left leg: the lower part of his leg was extending at an obscene angle. It was a major break; the bone had been completely snapped. To repair the fracture, the doctors had to insert a large plate and pins and then put Bill in a cast that extended from his hip to his toes. He was told that he would be in the hospital for a week or more.

"We were distressed for him, but to be honest we were also distressed for ourselves: this meant the end of a long-cherished plans. Bill, however, would hear nothing about ending our holiday over a mere broken leg! He ordered us out -- positively demanding that we continue on our way to Los Angeles. He promised that he would join us there as soon as he got out of the hospital. And so he did. We had a marvellous holiday in California and then a great drive back to Port Arthur -- although one that was a bit unusual with three of us packed into the front seat and Bill stretched out across the back, his cast out the open window."

Bill always loved risk and adventure; he enjoyed living "on the edge". After his discharge from the air force and before he was married, he and a buddy from his high school years had bought a 1937 Nash which they had proceeded to use as though it were a street rod.

"In the winter, Bill had great fun taking the Nash out onto the ice of Lake Superior, driving full tilt at the breakwater, then slamming on the brakes and throwing the car into reverse so that it would twirl like a top. He, of course, kept the doors open in case he hit a patch of weak ice.

"In the end, however, it was not ice but gravity that killed the Nash. Late one night, Bill was driving down the Waverley Street hill, perhaps a bit too quickly, and put his foot on the brake pedal. The pedal went straight to the floor! With an intersection looming ahead, Bill took the wise way out, veered through a high board fence and slammed the Nash against a tree. Bill walked away unharmed, but the old Nash never moved again under its own power."

* * * * * * *

In these same years, Bill was also becoming known as a man who loved people. He earned the gratitude of many people by "walking the second mile" for them, going far beyond what they had ever expected or asked of him. In many cases, they hadn't even needed to ask. The following is typical.

"My most vivid memories of Bill revolve around the way in which he came to help my husband and me even though he scarcely knew us. My husband was a chronic alcoholic, a man who really tried very hard to recover from this disease but who never made it. Repeatedly, he would go on insane binges and these would inevitably end in his being hospitalised with the DT's. In those years, there were no clinics as we have them today. Drunks were put on the wards of general hospitals, but their families were required to stay at their bedsides night and day to hold them and quiet them as they went through their shakes and heaves and hallucinations.

"My husband and I knew Bill only casually, but somehow Bill heard one time about what we were going through. Without his being asked, he appeared at the door of the hospital room. After introducing himself, he said to me, 'You go home and get some rest; I'll stay here.'

I thought that he meant he would sit for an hour or two. 'No,' he said, 'I've got my toothbrush. I'll stay all night' He was still there, sitting beside the bed, when I returned in the morning.

"And that was the first of many, many nights and many, many times that Bill spent, sparing me and caring for my husband. Sometimes, he would bring along a friend to sit with him; sometimes, he came alone. He tried to help my husband during the sober spells, but that was for nought. My husband died in an alcoholic haze. I was the one whom Bill really helped. I don't know how I could have survived without him."

****

Describing the sort of man Bill was before 1963, those who knew him best remember one other rare quality which he had in abundance. Despite his willingness to act whenever needed and despite his penchant for living all of life "full out", he also always seemed to be calm, controlled, at peace within himself. In a well known verse, a poet praises the man "who can keep his head when all about are losing theirs". Bill was such a man. He didn't panic in the face of danger. He didn't despair when things went wrong,; he was always able to accept life as it came and to "keep on keeping on." Many of us who came to know Bill only after 1963 marvelled at this deep sense of quiet which he carried and conveyed, and we attributed this gift to his spiritual awakening. Some of us were dismayed that, in comparison with Bill's life, our own lives remained so restless and turbulent. Perhaps our dismay was at least in part unwarranted: in this department of life, Bill seems to have had a head start on most of us. Certainly the events of 1963 deepened and amplified Bill's gift of inner peace -- but Bill had some of that gift even before God took over his life: he seems to have been born with it.

* * * * * * *

What about the problem of Bill's drinking? Some who have heard about Bill and who are now reading this book may be asking that question. "What about Bill's alcohol problem?" In 1962, most people who knew Bill would have responded, "What problem?" Certainly, Bill and his family saw no problem. The drinking which had begun in the air force had continued. Both he and Marion were social drinkers; frequently, wine was on the table with the evening meal; beer was always in the refrigerator. At times, Bill drank a bit heavily; occasionally, he drank too much. But he was never intoxicated in public; he never brought disgrace on the family name; he was never arrested for driving while over the limit. Drinking didn't seem to be interfering with the good things of his life. There are still members of Bill's family who cannot understand why he chose eventually to label himself an alcoholic; they wonder if his choosing to say that he was an alcoholic was not in fact an unconscious attempt on his part to identify himself with those whom he wanted to help: much as Jesus chose to be baptized among the sinners, did Bill choose to be counted among the alcoholics?

* * * * * * *

And so we see Bill in 1963, a happily married man, a father of three children, a partner in a thriving family business, a son of a highly respected family, a member of the church and chairman of the 'Y', given to helping others but still very much a "man's man", enjoying the good things of life, sports, friendships, and reckless fun. Apart from Marion's strange illness, there does not seem to be a cloud on his horizon. And yet, despite his outward success and his appearance of inward calm, Bill is dimly aware that something is wrong; though he doesn't know what it is, he senses that something important is missing.

CHAPTER TWO

THE SURRENDER

In the autumn of 1962, St. Paul's United Church in Port Arthur took a new direction. For the remainder of 1962 and throughout the three and a half years that followed, the primary emphasis was switched from social issues and Christian education to "life-changing" and the need for personal conversion. Worship services and adult study groups focused largely on the need to get one's life straightened out with God by making a personal and complete surrender to Christ. "Let go and let God!" "New lives for old!" "Change through Christ!" These became the slogans of faith in St. Paul's.

(This "life-changing" approach to Christianity had its roots in the Oxford Group, begun after the First World War. Its founder, an American Lutheran pastor named Frank Buchman, had devised a spiritual formula which could produce a radical change of character in those men and women who wholeheartedly took the steps recommended[4]. The procedure involved the following:

(1) the open admission of one's personal sin and failure and a readiness to stop trying to run one's own life;

(2) the yielding of every area of one's life to the God revealed in Christ, allowing that understanding of God to control every detail;

(3) the making of a spiritual and moral inventory in which one records every act and habit which troubles one's conscience;

(4) using the inventory as a basis for confession, an absolutely frank sharing with another person of the exact nature of one's wrongs and weaknesses;

(5) a readiness to confess and to make full restitution wherever possible to those whom one

---

[4] The movement became nicknamed the "Oxford Group" because one of the first places in which it gained a strong following was Oxford University in England. (The Oxford Group had no connection whatever with the "Oxford Movement" in the Church of England in the Nineteenth Century.) Following the Second World War, the Oxford Group changed its name to "MRA: Moral Re-Armament".

has wronged;

(6) through prayer and meditation, a daily "listening" for God's guidance and plans for one's life;

(7) a willingness to live (by God's grace), following four ideals: absolute honesty, absolute chastity, absolute love, and absolute unselfishness.

(8) a readiness at all times and under all circumstances to share with others the new life one has received, being willing to assist them in their own spiritual journeys.

Between the two world wars, the Oxford Group spread across Europe and North America; thousands of cell groups were established, meeting in private homes. (In the mid-ninteen-thirties, it was through just such a cell group in Akron, Ohio, that "Bill W." and "Dr. Bob" were brought together to form Alcoholics Anonymous; and A.A. (and, indeed, all other Twelve Step Programs) still acknowledge their indebtedness to Frank Buchman and the life-changing approach of his Oxford Group.) Several cells of the Oxford Group had been established in the Ottawa area during World War II, and it was a member of one of these Ottawa cells who had introduced this new emphasis to St. Paul's in 1962.

Quickly, the new approach took root within the congregation. The effects were quite dramatic. Attendance at worship and stewardship contributions greatly increased; a second morning service and evening services were established. Eight Bible fellowship groups were begun within homes of the congregation; new social groups were organized to attract both adults and 'teenagers into the church. Morning worship services were broadcast to a large listening audience. Weekend retreats were held for the elders and their spouses. Holy Week missions brought large congregations to evangelistic services. A new pipe organ had already been purchased, and now before its installation the church sanctuary was totally renovated. Amid all these activities, however, the most important fact lay in the lives that were being changed. Every month saw three or four more people (and sometimes many more), declaring that Jesus had become their Lord and then beginning to live lives which proved that their claim was indeed true.

Many of the members and families, long established within St. Paul's, were more than a little puzzled over what was happening in their church. Sometimes, words like "extremism" and even "fanaticism" were whispered. But there was no denying that the congregation was filled with high enthusiasm, generous stewardship, and new activities. And there was no denying that those whose lives were being "changed", far from becoming extremists or fanatics, were living sane, sober, exemplary lives. By 1963, St. Paul's had about eighty families that could be regarded as "changed" (within a congregation of nine hundred families): a spiritual renewal was underway within the congregation.

Bill had witnessed several of his friends undergoing this experience of change, and he had been impressed. He was particularly impressed by the difference he saw in one man. Ten years previously, this gentleman had made a life-commitment to Christ during a men's retreat in Muskoka; now, he had renewed that commitment and had made that renewal known to his friends. Bill had long admired this man and had found in his life a quality which he had envied but had never been able to define. Now, as he heard his friend's testimony about the difference Jesus makes in a person's life, Bill began to sense what it was that was missing in his own life.

As was noted at the end of the last chapter, Bill by all worldly standards was enjoying a very successful life. Husband, father, business partner, sportsman, he seemed to have it all "made" -- but beneath that exterior, there were problems. There was, of course, Marion's still undiagnosed illness. Then, too, there was his work in the family business, a position which provided less satisfaction than he would have liked. Above all, there was within him that "God-shaped vacuum" that affects so many, that hunger for God, that spiritual restlessness which, as St. Augustine describes it, "allows us no rest until we find our rest in God." Secretly, too, Bill knew that he was drinking heavily, too heavily; his doctors had warned him that he was going to lose much of his stomach and might lose his life if he didn't cut back on his alcohol intake. Bill had several times tried to stop or to cut back but had found that that was "easier said than done"; repeatedly he had ended up drinking more than he had wanted, more than he knew was wise. He was having difficulty sleeping, and he had begun to take such products as *Hoffman Drops* from the pharmacy shelves. And Marion now had prescription drugs in the house. By 1962, doctors were prescribing tranquillizers and anti-depressants for her; Bill was sometimes combining these with alcohol. Yet here he saw about himself several friends, and especially this one long-admired man, all of them living lives that radiated happiness, peace, confidence. Bill was genuinely puzzled: these men said that they knew Christ -- but how could anyone know someone who had died twenty centuries earlier?

     In the spring of 1963, Bill began to go to the minister of St. Paul's with his questions; the minister recalls those meetings.

"Bill's office was only a few blocks from the church; and on a regular basis, two or three times a week, Bill would 'phone me mid-morning and ask if I would be free for lunch. He would arrive with some sandwiches in a brown paper bag, and the two of us would spend the noon hour, eating at my desk, and discussing life and death in general, God and Jesus in particular. I very much enjoyed these sessions with Bill; they were pleasure rather than work for me. Only much later, looking back over Bill's life, did I come to realize that these meetings with Bill were perhaps the most important events taking place in my ministry at St. Paul's.

"Wherever our conversations began, Bill would always steer them to the question of what was happening in the lives of his friends. What did it mean to enter the Kingdom of God? How could a man make God his King? How could a person know God's will? How could God speak to a human soul? I remember telling Bill repeatedly that he was making things too complicated. 'The surrender of one's life to God is a simple step; just give up running your life and hand it over to God -- He'll take it from there.' Bill couldn't or wouldn't believe it was that easy.

"I remember advising Bill, too, that if he ever did make this great decision, to let me or someone else know. Secret commitments so easily peter out. Bill needed to 'drive in a stake' so that he would never be able to back out! (That shows how little I knew about Bill at the time. I didn't realize that Bill was a man who would never back out of any commitment he had made to anyone, least of all a commitment to God! Bill's word was always his bond.)"

After many weeks of such conversations, Bill made the decision which was to change his life and which, through his influence, was eventually to affect thousands of others across Canada and the United States. The minister continues,

"Early one afternoon, after one of our noon hour sessions, the phone rang at the church. It was Bill, back at the drug store. 'I'm doing as you instructed,' he said; 'I stopped at the funeral home on my way back to the office, went into the chapel there, and gave my entire life to Jesus. But nothing seems to be happening. I don't feel any different.' 'Don't worry, Bill,' I assured him, "if your life now belongs to Christ, you are different -- and you'll know it soon enough.

"The next morning, Bill was at the door of the manse before I had finished breakfast. Bill wasn't a demonstrative person; he didn't express his feelings very openly. That morning, however, he was truly excited. 'This is great! ' he exclaiming, 'What's happening to me?' I told him the simple truth that God had taken up residence within him."

* * * * * * *

With God "in residence", Bill's life underwent an extreme and rapid renovation. With the same sort of abandon with which he schussed the ski slopes, he plunged into his new commitment. Naturally, there were questions and misunderstandings. His brothers and business partners, George and Jamie, didn't know what to make of the "new Bill". They felt that he was carrying this "religion business" far too far -- not that he tried to involve them personally: they simply observed the way in which Bill's surrender of his life was beginning to express itself in service to the Church and to others, service that was so generous and wholehearted that they worried for Marion and the three children. What impact would Bill's decision have on them?

Marion, of course, was the person most deeply affected and the person who observed most closely the changes that were taking place in Bill. That she was perturbed is to put it mildly. She asked the minister to come to the house one afternoon.

"When I entered the living room, I sensed that Marion was not happy with me. It was apparent that she was holding me responsible for Bill's new way of life. She was puzzled, worried, concerned that Bill was going overboard. She wondered why all this 'extremism' was considered necessary; she had spent all her life within the Church and had never heard anything about people needing to make radical changes in their lives. And yet Marion was so sweet and open, and wanted so much to understand what this conversion business was all about.

"I explained that I had done nothing to Bill; Bill had simply opened his life to God, and God had entered. There was nothing that she or I could do to change that fact. I went on to tell her about a friend of mine who had resisted the changes he saw in his wife when she had surrendered her life to God. This man had said that it was like seeing his wife standing aboard a ship that was sailing out of the harbour: he knew that either he, too, would have to get on board or his wife would be lost to him forever.

"Some weeks later, Bill told me that Marion had 'come on board'. She became as deeply committed in her faith as he was in his. What a difference it made to Bill that his life partner was with him in all that he undertook for God! And what a difference it made in Marion! She so often said that she could not have survived the events that were soon to overtake her had she not put her life into the hands Christ!"

****

No one seems to remember how Bill became involved in A.A. As was mentioned at the beginning of this chapter, the "Twelve Steps" of A.A. were derived from the approach of the Oxford Group; and it was that approach which underlay the "spiritual renewal" which Bill had observed among his friends at St. Paul's -- an admission of total defeat, an unconditional surrender to God, a confession of sin and a willingness to make restitution, a reordering of one's life, and a daily search for God's guidance: in short, letting go of one's life and letting God take over. Of course, this pattern for living had not begun with the Oxford Group: Two thousand years earlier, Jesus had told His followers,

> "Seek first the Kingdom of God and His righteousness and all these things will be added unto you." In other words, "Make God your King, give Him absolute obedience, make His will for your life your only concern, and do only those things which you know are right and good in His sight -- and all that you need, (not all that you want but all that you need), will come to you."

The "Big Book" of A.A. echoes that promise:

> "See to it that your relationship with God is right, and great events will come to pass for you.... Abandon yourself to God as you understand God. Admit your faults to Him and to your fellows. Clear away the wreckage of your past. Give freely of what you find and join us. ... You will surely meet some of us as you trudge the Road of Happy Destiny."

* * * * * * *

As this book was being put together, someone raised the question, "Was Bill ever really 'in A.A.'?" There was a moment of stunned silence and then an explosion of laughter. "Was Bill ever in A.A.? Why Bill's whole life was A.A.! He lived and breathed A.A.!" From that day in the funeral chapel when he had turned his life over to God, Bill was on that "road to happy destiny" of which the "Big Book" speaks. Bill understood God in terms of Jesus, and so it was "Christ" whom he trusted and served -- but Bill's discipleship to Jesus was expressed through the Twelve Steps which he accepted and followed without reservation. So many people were to marvel at Bill's way of life. They asked about his "secret", but there was no "secret" -- only such simple steps as these that follow.

* * * * * * *

Step One: "We admitted we were powerless over alcohol and that our lives had become unmanageable."

Bill's victories stemmed from his surrenders. His strength lay in the fact that he fully realized his weakness; he admitted his powerlessness, his inability to run his own life or the lives of others. He had discovered that he could not handle his growing dependence on alcohol and drugs and so he stopped struggling with that issue; on his own, he knew, he was beaten. But this admission of powerlessness extended into all other parts of his life. He acknowledged that he could not handle the strange disease which was slowly overtaking Marion and affecting their marriage; his worry in that department was accomplishing nothing; he was powerless over what lay ahead for his family.

Nor could Bill avoid a growing sense that his work within the family firm was becoming sterile and unsatisfying for him, but with three children to support and with only a Grade Ten diploma, what else could he do? Nothing! In this as in all situations, he was powerless.

This admission of powerlessness, this acknowledgment that he was unable to solve the problems or come up with the right answers was at the heart of Bill's new life. Jesus speaks of the necessity of humbling ourselves and becoming like "little children" before we can enter the Kingdom of God. Throughout the years that followed his conversion, Bill continued to live with a childlike humility, confessing his powerlessness, turning every situation over to God. One of his friends, a counsellor who worked in one of his clinics, writes,

"I have never known anyone who was as conscious of his own inadequacy and weakness as was Bill. Step One of A.A. was the foundation of all his strength and success. His serenity was rooted in his practice of surrendering to God all those things that he knew he could not control, all those situations that he could not change.

"Bill knew that, if he took charge of his own destiny or tried to solve life's problems by his own wisdom and

strength, he would end up either in a ditch or in a head-on collision. He, therefore, climbed into the back seat and let God do the driving. As problems and crises, both professional and personal, came to him, he simply turned them over to his Higher Power because he knew that he, by himself, could not handle them.

"So often I have heard him say, 'Quit trying to manage your life. Surrender! Admit you're beaten!' He would summarise the first three steps of A.A. in three simple phrases, 'I can't. God can. So let Him.' That was Bill's secret: he really knew that he couldn't -- and so he let God."

* * * * * * *

That brings us to another step and another key element in Bill's spiritual journey:

Step Three: "We made a decision to turn our will and our lives over to the care of God as we understood Him.

Many of us claim to have surrendered our wills to God; but, if examined closely, our spiritual commitments turn to have all sorts of strings attached. We will proceed with our discipleship -- but only so far. We will go where Christ may lead us -- but not in certain directions. "Lord, we will follow you -- but first . . ." As was acknowledged in the introduction to this book, Dwight Moody was almost right in his assertion that the world has never seen a person who will give himself completely to the service of God. Only very rarely is a person's life completely surrendered to God -- but, as was said in that introduction, there have been some totally committed souls who are the exceptions to Moody's generalisation. Bill was one of them. Again, an observer tells us about it:

> "Usually, when people make the decision to give their lives to God, they do so in general terms; Bill, however, seemed to make the surrender in very specific terms. He sat down and counted the cost of discipleship. He didn't give only his 'life' to God: he gave his home, his marriage, his children, his relationships, his work, his time, his money, his future. He didn't simply give God a mortgage on his life; he gave Him a chattel mortgage on all that he had, all that he was. Put quite simply, Bill's life was no longer Bill's life. It had been given to God in every detail."

Step Three speaks of "turning our wills and lives over to the care of God *as we understood Him.*" Bill understood God in terms of Jesus of Nazareth; he was profoundly committed to Christ. To Bill, the question, "What does God want done?", always meant, "What would Jesus do?" Unlike many zealous Christians, however, Bill never tried to impose his understanding of God on other people; he never wanted to argue theology or to concern himself with religious doctrines. To him, the spiritual life was like climbing up a mountain to reach the summit. He knew that for him Jesus was the way to the top; but, if others were climbing by a different route, he was not concerned. That they were climbing was all that mattered. There was no need to stop and argue about the way to get to the top; Bill reckoned that, the closer a person came to the summit, the more he would find the pathways all converging Those who wanted to stop and debate the merits of various routes weren't climbing.

A woman writes about her spiritual encounter with Bill:

> "I came out of a "church-centered" home, with two parents who took their Christianity quite seriously and their Bible quite literally. As I became an adult, however, I found that the Christian approach to God was far too rigid and narrow for me. Eventually, through contacts with various meditation groups based on Hindu concepts, I found a spiritual interpretation of life which was at that time more meaningful to me.

"I was, nevertheless, having difficulties with alcohol and with depression, and it was suggested by friends that I meet Bill Crooks, a man who had been of help to them. I had already heard about Bill. I knew that he was a very dedicated Christian, and so I had mixed feelings about going to see him: I was worried that he might want to persuade me to return to my Christian roots.

"I began the meeting by telling Bill about my new 'understanding of God', how I had come to believe that God is hidden within all forms of life, how all life is sacred, how the purpose of life is to discover the Divine that lies inside us, and so forth. I told him about the concepts of karma and reincarnation which I found so intriguing.

"Bill didn't argue. He listened politely. He said to me, 'That's neat! Now let's talk about how your understanding of God can be put to work.' You didn't come here to discuss religious philosophy with me. Let's look at your real problem. What's been going on in your life?"

"Years later, I began a study of the New Testament; and in the Gospel according to St. John, I came upon that story of

Jesus' meeting with the woman of Samaria. She had wanted to debate matters of theology with Jesus, and Jesus had brushed that aside and had pointed out that her real problem lay much deeper. In her case, whatever her concept of God, if she wanted to know God, she had to start by looking at her relationships with men. I realized that that had been Bill's approach with me; he had forced me to go beyond all my religious philosophising, cut to the chase, and face those real issues in my life that I had chosen to avoid.'"

* * * * * * *

Bill turned his life and will over to the care of God -- but how was God able to communicate His care to Bill? As later stories in this book will indicate, Bill developed an uncanny sense of God's guidance and direction, but whence did this come? Another one of the Twelve Steps provides us with much of the answer:

Step Eleven: "We sought through prayer and meditation to improve our conscious contact with God as we understood Him, praying only for knowledge of His will for us and the power to carry that out.

From the outset of his new spiritual adventure, Bill recognized the power of prayer and his utter need of that power if he hoped to live a new life. He had no illusions that he could live a godly life without God's guidance and strength. He established the pattern of beginning each day with readings from the Bible (often accompanied by a devotional commentary to guide his thoughts.) Then would follow a time of prayer and "listening". He believed that, in these quiet times, if he were ready to obey, God would tell him what he must do. At first, the guidance had been very general, perhaps little more than a confirmation of what Bill already knew should be done. As he grew in the spiritual life, however, and as he became obedient in fulfilling the simple tasks which had been set before him, Bill began to receive quite specific instructions -- the name and 'phone number of someone he had to see, or the knowledge that he should visit a certain family at a certain time. On scraps of paper, Bill would jot down these "daily marching orders".

Many of us regard prayer and meditation as sombre and serious activities; we feel vaguely uncomfortable when we think of "Bible study" and "devotions". To Bill, however, these were simple and straightforward, as enjoyable and essential as eating breakfast in the morning; they were a regular part of his daily routine. One man, a recovering alcoholic, stayed with Bill and Marion for several weeks while he was unemployed and was searching for work in Thunder Bay. He observed Bill's "quiet times".

"At this point in my life, I was anything but 'spiritual'. Prayer was a meaningless 'mumbo-jumbo'. But I needed Bill to get a ride downtown each morning, and so I would get up when I heard his alarm go off, always before dawn and long before the rest of the family was awake. We would have breakfast together (usually fried eggs and toast), and then we'd take our coffee into the living room, he to pray and I to read the newspaper.

"What struck me was how natural were Bill's "quiet times". There was nothing pious or phony about them. I remember him sitting in an arm chair by the window, a cup of coffee in one hand, his Bible in another. Then he would read some devotional book -- (I think it was some A.A. publication.) And then he would be very quiet, with his eyes closed. Eventually, he would open his eyes, take a piece of paper and write a few sentences -- and then look at me and ask, 'Ready for another coffee?' He never seem embarrassed that I was there, nor did he ever try to push me into praying with him. He must have known that I wasn't ready for that yet. But by his example, Bill was showing me the secret of spiritual success."

* * * * * * *

Step Eleven made possible Step Twelve, the step that was the essence of Bill's life:

Step Twelve: "Having had a spiritual awakening as a result of these steps, we tried to carry this message to alcoholics and to practice these principles in all our affairs."

Bill lived the Twelfth Step; he practised the principles of honesty, humility, and unselfishness in all his life -- and no one has ever tried harder than did he to carry the message of new life and new hope, not just to other alcoholics, but to everybody who was in any kind of suffering or need. From the moment his Higher Power took over his life, Bill was under a compulsion to serve, to help, to give; his life was no longer his, but God's. And, with the same reckless courage that marked all else that he did, Bill plunged into his work for God.

There are hundreds upon hundreds of stories that could be told about Bill at this point -- far too many for a little book like this. Doubtless, many of the greatest stories will never be told: Bill never spoke of them, and they are now known only to God and to the individuals whom he helped. The accounts that come in the following chapters, however, will give some sense of how Bill, while remaining very much a "man's man" a family man, a business man, a sportsman, was now turning into "God's gentleman", a friend to all who needed him, someone who made a vital difference in so many lives.

CHAPTER THREE

IN THE SERVICE OF LOVE

Having had his spiritual awakening in the Church, Bill all his life remained strongly committed to the Church. Wherever they lived, at first in Port Arthur and then later in the United States, he and Marion forged strong links with local congregations; they did so, not only because they believed they needed the inspiration and the fellowship of being with their fellow Christians but because they saw the special opportunities for witness and service which churches provided. Marion's continuing illness curtailed what she could do outside the home[5], but Bill accepted every duty and responsibility that the Church laid on him, whether serving as a steward or an elder,

---

[5] One special ministry to which Marion gave herself unstintingly was "reading for the blind". Through Lakehead University, she obtained lists of the text books and reference works which were required reading in key courses, and she carefully recorded these on tape for the visually handicapped students on that campus. The books were often long and dull, but Marion made the reading a priority in her weekly schedule.

whether heading a financial drive or organizing hospital visitations. And, if he saw an opportunity which a congregation was missing, he would take it upon himself to correct the situation; his work with teens is a good example. The minister of St. Paul's recalls how Bill's "conversion" had a major impact upon many of the young people in that church.

"**Although a kind of spiritual renewal was at work in St. Paul's, the toughest challenge was to reach the 'teens. Then as now, young people did not consider it 'cool' to be interested in anything of which parents might approve. Thus, we had an extremely large Sunday School -- but, as soon as the young people entered high school, we began losing them right, left, and centre.**

"**I was approached by Bill and the man whose witness and way of life had so intrigued him. The two of them wanted to start a new sort of Bible fellowship group for 'teens. (I was delighted but surprised for few people voluntarily enlist for Christian Education work and very few of those who do are young business men.) These two men believed they could make a difference.**

"**I was astonished at what happened. Although there were only four young people the first Sunday morning, that** number steadily grew -- eight, twelve, sixteen, twenty. At first, we had to keep bringing more chairs into the room. Then, it became necessary to start removing the chairs in order to make space for still more young people. Eventually, the room was packed, with 'teens and the two leaders all sitting on the floor.

"I was curious about the attraction: how were Bill and his friend bringing so many into their program? When I asked, however, I found that there was no special 'catch'. The young people were simply recognizing that these men were sharing with them something that they themselves had experienced, something that had made all the difference in their own lives. In Bill and his friend, the 'teens saw genuine proof that knowing God makes all the difference in a person's life."

Several of these 'teens began thinking in terms of entering the Christian ministry. One of them who now is minister of a Congregational church in Southern Ontario writes of how he believes so many young lives were changed.

"At the time I began attending the Sunday morning fellowship, I still had not yet accepted Christ, but I was very drawn to Him by these two men. They had a quality about them that was so attractive. I couldn't put my finger on it at the time, but now I know that it was the love of Jesus coming through them to us. I hadn't experienced that kind of love before: here were two "ordinary" guys who were taking time to teach a Bible class -- and it was obvious that they were doing so because they really loved us kids. They were interested in our lives, our problems at home or school. They were happy to talk with us at any time. They often had us to their homes.

"Later, after Christ had taken over my life, they started a more advanced study group with six of us, all 'teenaged boys. We met one night a week at Bill's home -- but because the house was always so busy, the only quiet place we could find was the master bedroom. There we met each week, sitting on the kitchen chairs with which we encircled the bed. We would start with prayer, and then would study and discuss a book by someone like Elton Trueblood or C. S. Lewis. We would report on what God had been doing in our lives in the week past, would share prayer requests for the week ahead, and then would pray for each other. It was a time of amazing spiritual growth for me; through these two men, I experienced the same sense of true 'Christian community' that we read about in the Acts of the Apostles.

"Then, when I went on my first mission field in 1968, I was sent to rural Manitoba. It was the first time that I had ever been entirely on my own. I was working with strangers. I often felt lonely and out of my depth. Invariably, at such moments, a letter would arrive from Bill. During his morning quiet time, he would have felt guided to write me. His letters were always encouraging, building me up in my faith, and helping me to carry on with confidence in the Lord.

"So Bill was an important part of my early Christian life. God used him greatly to help a young, shy, uncertain 'teen begin to walk securely in a personal relationship with Christ. Thanks be to God!"

The minister who was at St. Paul's in the early nineteen-sixties tells of the regard in which Bill Crooks was held by the 'teenagers of the congregation:

"I overheard a 'bull session' that took place among four or five of the boys in the church. They had been studying the

Sermon on the Mount and were debating among themselves how literally one can take Christ's teachings about turning the other cheek, walking the second mile, living without anger or lust, and so forth. One of the boys came to the same conclusion that many adults have reached, that the teachings are unrealistic in their idealism. 'No one can live that way!' he said, 'It's impossible!'

"But another boy asked, 'Then what about Jesus? He lived that way!' There was a murmur of dissent; 'Jesus was special. Jesus was different. Jesus was not an ordinary man.' Then the questioner raised a second example, "Okay, then what about Bill Crooks?' This time, there was no dissent but rather a nodding of heads.

"Listening to this, I found it remarkable that, however he had done it, this man was living the new life so convincingly that these 'teenagers were persuaded that it was possible to follow Christ's teachings completely."

* * * * * * *

In the same way, Bill used his contacts within a congregation to discover situations in which his help was needed. Sometimes, this led to problems. Again, the former minister of St. Paul's remembers.

"After his commitment of his life to God, one of the first tasks which we gave Bill was oversight of the Benevolent Fund, a small fund made up of offerings given for the relief of situations of special need which came to the church's attention.

"After a time, I began to hear reports of all the wonderful work being done through the Benevolent Fund. I received many unexpected letters of thanks from people we had helped, people about whom I knew nothing. I inquired and discovered that Bill was not waiting for people to come and make requests; on his own, he was searching for people with special needs, going out of his way to find those whom he could help.

"This approach made the task impossibly large; I knew that our Benevolent Fund was very limited. I wondered how on earth Bill was making our money stretch so far. The answer was simple: he was using his own money. In fairness to his family, I turned the Benevolent Fund over to someone else and hoped that Bill would not always feel that he was personally responsible for the needs of the whole world."

Removing Bill from his official "benevolent responsibilities" did not, however, end his concern for those in need, and always that concern expressed itself in practical action. When he heard about someone who was in difficulty, Bill never shrugged and said, "That's too bad." Action, not sympathy, was needed. Bill's response was always, "Let's do something about it." Bill's contacts with the church brought him reports of need, and those same contacts with the church also provided him with solutions to need: Bill often marshalled his church friends to help him in this work. One Sunday, for example, following the morning worship, Bill was having an "after-service" cup of coffee when someone mentioned a family in the city, (a family having no connection with the church), who were being evicted from their apartment. The husband had lost his job; the rent was several months overdue; there were two small children; another was expected shortly. Someone tells what then happened.

"As others turned to more coffee and cookies, Bill asked about the address of the family; shortly afterwards, he left the church. Around suppertime, he appeared at my house, wanting to talk.

"It turned out that he had gone immediately from the church to the apartment. He had more or less invited himself in. He had met the family, had

asked the husband and wife about their situation, and had been convinced that the story he had heard was true and that the need was genuine. He had inquired about the man's work experience and then had left and gone to see El Whitney.

"El is now retired; but, at the time of this story, he was a grain trimmer at the big elevators in the Lakehead harbour. He, too, is a dedicated Christian; he had often found jobs in the elevators for men with whom Bill was working. On this day, El made some 'phone calls and arranged things so that Bill's new friend would have employment within a few days.

"Bill had then gone to see the family's landlord and with some difficulty had persuaded him to agree to rescind the eviction notice provided that the overdue rent was paid immediately. Bill's own bank account was stretched, and so he had come to me, asking me to put up the money, offering his personal guarantee that it would be repaid. I was glad to do so.

"Bill returned to the landlord with my cheque in his hand and settled the rent issue; he then went to the apartment to tell the family that they could stay in their home and that a job had been secured for the husband.

"And then, around 8 p.m., Bill went home for dinner. Apart from his noon coffee following morning worship, he had had nothing since breakfast. And probably Bill said nothing to anyone about what he had been doing; if asked, he would have said simply that he had been "busy". Bill never wanted anyone to know."

* * * * * * *

Take a story like that and multiply it over and over again: only then can one begin to realize how remarkable was this "man who made a difference." Bill's outreach was soon extending far beyond his contacts in St. Paul's United Church. All across the Lakehead, people with problems began to hear about a man in a Port Arthur company who set no limits on what he would do to help others. People began arriving at Crooks' to make appointments to see Bill; sometimes downstairs, outside his basement office, there would be two or three waiting in line to tell him their problems. His home on Rupert Street became another drop-in centre to which people came at all hours of the day and night. Of course, Bill became regarded as a "soft touch", an "easy mark". Loans were sometimes not repaid; promises were sometimes broken; generosity was sometimes answered with ingratitude. Bill never lost faith.

* * * * * * *

What of Bill's family in all this? Marion was a committed Christian and was fully supportive of all that he was doing; but many have remarked that she had to have had the patience of a saint to have had Bill forever being pulled away from her. Night after night, dinners were interrupted by 'phone calls or left uneaten as Bill left the table to meet someone in distress. Peter, the older son, describes how eventually, not just Marion, but the whole family came to sense that Bill was busy with the important things of God:

> "When my father first made his commitment to Christ, it didn't seem like such a big deal to me. I was at an age when I regarded such a step as being a bit fanatical; now, of course, I understand what an immense decision this was for him. He didn't talk much about it to Paul, Carol, and me -- although I remember that, when my mother made the same commitment not long afterwards, she shared with us completely what it meant to her.
>
> "My parents' involvement in young people's work made a deep impression on me. I sometimes had difficulty with

this when I heard them talking to my peers about their personal faith; but after a year or so, my embarrassment turned to pride as I came to realize that their faith had not made them weird but rather had turned them into really nice people whom everybody seemed to love.

"There was a steady stream of visitors at 116 Rupert Street, people coming with various problems, some to stay for an hour, some to stay overnight, some to stay for weeks or even months. At first, these strangers in our midst felt like real intruders to my sister, brother, and me; but we got used to it. I guess that, since I was the oldest, I was the first to realize how much good was really being done and how many people were being rescued from deep trouble. And again I took a deep pride in what my 'not so normal' parents were doing for God."

Consider some of the following stories. Here's what "Lucille" tells of the way in which Bill (and Marion) rescued her. She was a high school student in a mill town on the north shore of Lake Superior, about a two hour drive from Thunder Bay. She was the daughter of a well known family in the town; her father was a high school teacher and served on the town council; her mother directed the choir in the community church. Lucy was their only child; great things were expected of her. Then, while she was in Grade 12, Lucy became too involved with one of her classmates A pregnancy resulted; the boy disclaimed any responsibility. Even today, such a situation is difficult for any girl to face; forty years ago in a small closely-knit company town, it was impossibly so! Lucy, herself, picks up the story.

"Suicide seemed the only way out, but I didn't know how to manage even that. I can't put into words how ashamed and frightened I felt. I didn't know what to do. I told no one! March break was coming, and so I took a bus to Port Arthur to spend ten days with Jo-Ann, one of my girl friends. As soon as I came off the bus, Jo-Ann knew that something was wrong. She soon guessed what it was; I swore her to secrecy.

"Jo-Ann told me about a church group she was attending; the leaders were both really understanding, she said. She asked me if I would see Bill. I cringed at the idea of a telling a stranger about the mess I was in; but, having no alternative, I agreed.

"Bill invited me to meet him for coffee in the restaurant beside his store. I remember how embarrassed I was and how gentle and reassuring he was. I kept saying that my situation was hopeless, and he kept telling me that he would do everything to help me find the right answer.

"Bill took me to his home to meet Marion. She was so accepting and so understanding. We talked for hours. They both prayed with me, asking for God's guidance. I refused their offer to speak with my parents on my behalf; whatever else, my family couldn't be told. I believed that the only answer was abortion. They felt that this was not the best solution, but I insisted.

"Bill made enquiries and discovered that an "abortion flight" to Sweden left Toronto once a month; the next flight was to be the following week. (Abortion was then illegal in Canada.) He arranged for my ticket and put it on his credit card. I went home to Terrace Bay, telling my parents some story about my plans to go Toronto the following week for a special youth conference.

"When I returned to Port Arthur all packed for my flights to Toronto and Sweden, Bill met me at the bus terminal and drove me to the airport. He gave me cash for my trip and told me how he had arranged for my passport to be waiting in

Toronto. He told me that Marion and he loved me. I began to cry and couldn't stop crying. I didn't want an abortion; I didn't want to go to far-off Sweden. We drove on to the airport where Bill cancelled my ticket; he then took me home to Marion.

"Within a day, while still staying at their house, I regretted the decision I had made. Again, panic and despair took over. I refused to listen to reason. I simply had to have an abortion. At that point, most people would have given up in exasperation -- but not the Crooks. Bill went to work again and spent hours on the 'phone. He learned that "abortion flights" regularly left Vancouver for Japan, and he booked me on one of these, again with his own credit card. He got information on the Tokyo clinic and reserved a place for me. He arranged to have my passport sent by courier to Port Arthur.

"Two days later, however, I was again in tears. I couldn't go through with all this. I didn't have the strength. It wasn't right. Again, Bill did not criticise me; he simply cancelled all the detailed arrangements he had made on my behalf. And he and Marion talked to me about the option of trusting God with the situation I was in, telling my parents, and having my baby.

In tears, I at last agreed.

"Bill drove me all the way to my home town, all the while assuring me that everything would be all right, guaranteeing that he and Marion would be on my side whatever might happen. When we got to the house, he came in with me and sat beside me while I told my parents what was wrong. He helped them to understand and accept what was happening to their only child. That day ended in hugs and love, and then in a long drive home for Bill.

"Bill 'phoned friends in the Toronto area and found a Christian couple, former members of St. Paul's, who had a spare room and were willing to take me into their home. Then, after I had moved there a few weeks later, he and Marion wrote and telephoned me regularly to keep up my spirits and to make sure that I knew that they loved me.

"To conclude this long story, I'll say simply that I had a baby girl and gave her up for adoption. I returned home, completed my high school education, and went on to university. After graduation, I moved far from Northwestern Ontario and so rather lost touch with Bill and Marion. I never forgot them, however,

and will never forget them. He, with his busy work schedule and with all his commitments in the community, and she, with her family responsibilities and with the disease that was sapping her life -- these are the two people who saved my life and made real to me God's love."

****

Many of those who turned to Bill for help were alcoholics. Since Bill acknowledged himself to be one of them, they knew that he understood their disease and so was able to realize how terrifyingly difficult for them was the prospect of a "dry" life. Then, too, Bill was able to cut through all their excuses, and alibis. "Will you knock it off! Let's get down to what's really bothering you!" And man-to-man, he would tell of how God had changed his life and of the life of freedom that was available to all who "let go and let God."

Alcoholics are notorious for their relapses; however good their good intentions, only a minority ever grasp the way of life which leads to contented sobriety. Despite sincere promises and noble resolutions, they return to their drinking. Bill often witnessed this tragedy: he had the frustrating experience of seeing many people "fall off the wagon", men and women on whom he had lavished great amounts of his time and care. And yet he never lost his patience with them. One man writes,

"I wish I could say that knowing Bill Crooks made the difference that rescued me from alcoholism. I can't. I'm still an active alcoholic, forever slipping off the 'the wagon'. What I remember most about Bill is that he never gave up on me, no matter how often I let him down.

"I don't know how many times I have found myself in a bar, realizing that I had 'done it again', that I hadn't any taxi fare, and that it wasn't safe for me to drive home. Had I been thinking clearly, I would have walked home. Instead, I'd 'phone Bill, knowing that, however late it was, he would pick me up, would take me either to my place or his and sober me up. And how many times he had to go to the jail to pay my bail!

"Even in my drunkenness, I was amazed that he never lost patience with me. Long after everyone else in the world had given up on me, long after I had given up on myself, Bill still kept believing that someday I would 'get the program'. 'Go back to Step One,' he kept telling me, 'Realize your powerlessness; stop running your life.' So far, I haven't been able to stick with that step; but I know that, wherever he now is, Bill is still urging me to take it."

A neighbour tells about observing the same remarkable patience.

"We were neighbours of the Crooks. We saw the change that came over Bill and Marion in 1963. In that change, we especially remarked on their willingness to try to help others, no matter what the circumstances.

"I remember that we were all at a big Christmas party and around 6.30 were just about to sit down to a delicious dinner. The telephone rang. Someone was in difficulty and needed Bill. To Bill, it didn't matter that he was at a party with friends or even that he was hungry and hadn't had dinner. We heard him say, 'Okay, I'll be right over.' He made his apologies and left.

"He returned shortly before midnight, just as the party was breaking up. He seemed tired and hungry; he still hadn't eaten. He never said where he had been or whom he had helped. I don't know if he ever even told Marion. That was the way with Bill."

* * * * * * *

Bill's willingness to help others extended to the most menial of tasks; he "took the towel" and truly made himself the servant of all. If he heard that someone had a lawn that needed mowing or a trench that needed to be dug, Bill would either recruit a friend or do it himself. He never waited to be asked. The following story, though more dramatic than most, is typical of Bill.

> "Bill worked with our son-in-law, "Tom", who was addicted both to alcohol and to pain killers. Bill spent many hours and many days and nights with Tom, befriending him, encouraging him, even after all the rest of us had pretty well washed out hands of him. Bill was always sure that God would someday work a miracle in Tom's life.
>
> "It didn't happen. One afternoon, Tom 'phoned Bill at his work to tell him that he was at home and that in a few moments he was going to kill himself; he wanted Bill to notify the authorities and to break the news to family. (Our daughter, Tom's wife, was out of the city for the day but would be returning in the evening.) Then Tom hung up. Bill dialled '911' and raced to the house, but it was too late. Tom had gone down to the basement and blown off much of his head with a shotgun.
>
> "Bill was a great help. He was more a minister to us than was our own minister

because he seemed to know exactly how we were feeling and what to say. One thing that most impressed me was the fact that, as soon as Tom's body had been removed and the police had verified that the death was a suicide, Bill went home, changed his clothes, and came back to the house. He spent the next hours scrubbing the basement, washing away every bit of the gruesome mess.

"Bill didn't know our family well. He owed Tom and our daughter nothing, and yet he undertook this terrible task simply because he wanted to make the death a little less awful for our daughter. For a long time, we never knew who had cleaned the basement; it was the police who told us."

* * * * * * *

There seemed to be no limits to Bill's love. If he heard of a need anywhere, he tried to find an answer even if that answer took his own time and resources.

"I nursed on the children's ward of the hospital nearest Bill's pharmacy. Somehow Bill had learned about Louie, a nine-year-old patient of ours, who had terminal cancer. Louie's mother was a single parent on welfare. There was nothing we could do for Louie except to keep him comfortable. The cancer was spreading rapidly.

"For some reason, Bill began to visit Louie. Many evenings, a little after 6, as soon as the store was closed, Bill would appear on the ward. He was a good-looking man with grey hair, always neatly dressed. I assumed that he was a relative, perhaps Louie's uncle; I couldn't imagine any other reason why he would visit so faithfully.

"Louie really looked forward to these visits at the end of the day. Bill would read to him. Sometimes, they played checkers or cards. Always, before Bill left, they would pray. Louie knew that he was not going to recover; sometimes, they spoke about death and about Louie's faith.

"When Louie died, several nurses went to the funeral chapel. We were the only ones there except for the minister and Louie's mother and Bill. Later we learned that Bill's work with the welfare committee at his church had introduced him to the sad situation; he had immediately taken it upon himself to become a "big brother" to a little boy who was dying."

* * * * * * *

It has been noted that Bill never waited to be asked for assistance. If he heard about a need anywhere, he prayed about it and asked God for guidance. Was there anything that he could do? If it seemed there was, he volunteered. Often, he had only himself to offer -- and the assurance that a person was not alone. The following story is typical.

"I came to a place in my life where I had lost everything. I had been fired from a fairly lucrative job, and the circumstances of my dismissal left such a cloud over my reputation that it was unlikely I would ever again find employment in my field. With my disgrace and loss of position, my wife had seized all our family assets and had moved more than one thousand miles away, taking our children with her and assuring me that I would never again see her or them. I had neither the financial resources nor the emotional strength to face her in a court battle. My friends had largely deserted me. I was beaten into the ground.

"One Sunday afternoon, there was a knock on the door of the small apartment I had rented. I was surprised to find Bill there. I knew him but not well. Years earlier, we had sometimes skied together. When my wife and I had attended church, we had occasionally met him and Marion there. Our relationship was very casual. I didn't know why he had come to see me.

"I invited him in. Soon he was gently coaxing from me the story of what had happened. I badly needed to unload and so I told him everything, both what I had done and what had been done to me. I was filled with remorse, self-pity, and above all despair. Again and again, I returned to the theme of my hopelessness and helplessness. I wallowed in the darkness. Bill just listened, now and again asking a question which probed even deeper into the hell I was in. He offered no pat answers. He had no simple solutions to offer.

"Then, out of the blue, he challenged me to arm wrestle with him. I was dumbfounded! He told me to take off my coat and join him at the table. I'm a fairly strong man, and I felt fairly confident that I could beat him -- but he wore me down; after a minute, he had my armed pinned under his. 'Again,' he ordered, and again after a brief struggle, he pinned me. 'Still again,' he ordered, and again he won. There were ten or more of these bouts until I was quite worn out. Then, with my arm still pinned under the full force of his, Bill said to me slowly and deliberately, making me take in every word, 'Jim, you can feel the strength in my arm. Now I want you to know this: every ounce of that strength is for you! You are not alone. I'm with you in your trouble. You're going to get through this.'

"I can't explain what happened within me at that moment. I just know that out of that experience I gained hope that somehow things would work out. I knew that I was not alone. And I wasn't alone; Bill was true to his word. He kept in touch with me. He shared his time. Often, he had me as a guest in his home. He introduced me to new friends. He acted as a mediator with my wife. And gradually, my life did begin to move in new directions. What did Bill give me? He gave me himself."

Again, a reader should remember that all these stories are but a fraction of those that could be told. Generous and caring even before his Christian commitment, Bill's decision to commit all that he knew of himself to all that he knew of God amplified that generosity and caring beyond measure. A reader should also remember that Bill did all that he did while he was holding down major responsibilities in the family business, was being a good father to three adolescent children, and was watching his wife slowly succumb to her crippling and still undiagnosed disease   With all this in mind, read now the testimony of a woman who knows that she owes her life to Bill and Marion. It best summarizes the miracle that began when Bill gave his whole life to Christ. The writer is Marion's niece, someone whom Bill and Marion came to regard as a daughter.

> "Bill Crooks had a profound influence on my life, not only because he saved it -- (though he did), but because he directed me on a course of spiritual awakening that I couldn't have navigated by myself. He was an inextricable part of my life for half a century. How blessed I was to have had him as my guide and mentor, the support (and sometimes the beneficial bane) of my existence! At every step I took, he was there to help shape the course of my life.
>
> "As a child, I spent treasured parts of my summers with the Crooks family; but it was not until I was 16 years old that I really started to know Bill: he was to be an integral factor in my life for the next ten years. Larger than life, Bill always seemed to know when my need was

greatest and to know, too, how to withdraw when I was able to meet life head-on by myself. Being weaned was at times a painful experience but he knew it was absolutely necessary for me to learn to live independently.

"I first lived with Bill and Marion when I was 6 and then again when I was 18; both times, they opened their arms to welcome and embrace me. At 6, I came to them because my father tragically had lost his life. At 18, I came to them again because I was on the way towards losing my own life.

"Later, when I was 42, with sons who were 14 and 12, I found myself reflecting on the fact that I could never do for others what Bill and Marion had done for me so long before. When Marion was 42, her children were 15, 11, and 10 -- and yet she welcomed me as an 18-year-old daughter. I marvel at her generosity. Bill and Marion accepted me as one of their family. I shared their cottage with them, was included in their ski membership, got my driver's license practising on their car, and shared the household chores with the younger children.

"Marion was at the centre of this amazing family -- Marion, with her joyful, loving heart and her forgiving nature. She never criticised me but always complimented me; and in so doing she kept inching the bar a little higher so that I wanted to keep on improving. One night, for example, I was late coming home; creeping silently through the house on bare feet, I thought I had made it safely. Then I glimpsed Marion, sitting alone in the dark kitchen. I could tell by her expression that she had been very worried. Her words were superfluous. I never broke curfew again. And I will never stop missing her.

"Bill and Marion loved me as though I were one of their own. They took me by the hand and ever so gently led me by the light of love to know Jesus for myself. They did it all without words. I moved in with them during Grade Twelve; that year, Marion drove me all the way to Fort William every morning so that I could complete my school year. Then, in the summer that followed, I enrolled in a business college. As the college was near his work, Bill drove me to my classes every day for that year.

"Those mornings with Bill made a deep impression. When I was ready to leave the house, I would always join Bill in the living room for a cup of coffee. Every morning, I would find him there sipping coffee and reading the Bible. Every morning, I would look at the Bible in his hand and wonder, "Why the Bible? Why not a newspaper?" Bill never mentioned his Bible study. He never suggested that I read the Bible. Bill would simply finish his reading, put down the Bible, and ask if I were ready to go.

"This daily routine mystified me. It made me curious. From about the age of 10, I had made stabs at reading the Bible; in fact, I had read and re-read the first four chapters of Genesis about two hundred times. But no one had ever suggested that I could begin with the New Testament. When finally I asked, Bill pointed me to that Thirteen Chapter of First Corinthians, to that great passage on love, a passage which started my passion for the writings of St. Paul. Bill pointed out that St. Paul was writing letters to his friends and that a lot of Paul's instructions and admonitions might have a real bearing on my own life. He gave me a Bible and a couple of prayer books, but never even asked if I used them.

"I was a 'teenager and a troubled one at that. There were few escapades and escapes in which I didn't become involved; if I was not at the centre of the trouble, then I was at least standing round the edge. I smoked; I drank; I broke curfew; I lost my temper; I knew everything; I felt sorry for myself; and for a time I wanted only to die. I was such a pathetically desperate kid. I wanted and needed to be saved more than anything. I was so wretched and desperate.

"Two events from my eventual rescue stand out in my memory. One is of my sitting in the study at St. Paul's United Church, pouring out my story to Bill's minister. The other is of my then going to the drugstore, looking up at Bill behind the pharmacy counter and simply saying, 'Hi!' That's all I said, but Bill looked into my eyes and knew immediately that I needed help. He left whatever he was doing, stepped down to my level, and put his arm around me, and walked with me out of the store. If he hadn't, if he had lectured me or scolded me or "put me on hold", my life wouldn't be the way that it is now.

"Through it all, I was blessed with the music of angels and always with Bill leading the chorus. When I was alone and lonesome in Vancouver, Bill and Marion paid for my way home. When I was unable to survive at home, Bill and Marion again took me into theirs. After I had attempted suicide, Bill And Marion took me in again. When I wanted to join the circus, Marion merely suggested that I might first want to prepare by taking dance lessons or gymnastics, When I announced that I was going to join Albert Schweitzer in Africa, Bill advised me to check into vaccination requirements and to start saving for the 'plane fare. When I decided that I was called to be an Anglican nun, they put me on a 'plane to Toronto and wished me Godspeed on my way. And when I told them that I was going to marry someone whom I had known for only two weeks, they helped plan the wedding and Bill gave me away. (Thereafter, I often teased Bill that he agreed to give me away because this was the only way he could see to get me out of his family's life.) The truth is, however, that he and Marion had the faith to know that my marriage was the right thing. Nor were they mistaken: my husband and I have had thirty-one happy years together. (And, while I didn't join the circus and never went to Africa, I have had close contact with the Anglican sisters in Toronto and have been an associate of the order for many years.)

"Business college was the first thing I had ever finished in my life -- although it took Bill to point out that fact to me. I had never seen the importance of finishing anything; I had felt that the importance of achievement was overrated. I had liked to believe that life should flow of its own accord; rather like lava, it should follow the easiest path even if it left destruction in its wake. To me, graduating from college didn't seem like such a big deal. Not so to Bill! For him, my completion of my course was a life event. He came to my graduation, bought me a present, and told me over and over how proud he was of me. For the first time in my life, someone made me realize that there was real value in finishing something and hitting one's target. From that point on, I began to set goals and strive for successful achievement. I began to depend on myself for a sense of my own worth. Over the years that followed, there were to be other accomplishments and other successes; but, as it turned out, Bill was the only person who ever attended any ceremony that recognized me for what I had done.

"During the years that I lived with Marion and Bill, I remember vividly Bill's being called out at all hours of the day or night. It would always begin with a 'phone ringing, followed by Bill's telling Marion that he had to go out for a while and that he didn't know when he would be back. Marion never questioned his leaving, nor did she try to hold him back. If Bill discovered that there were young people involved in the family situations with which he was presented, he would sometimes enlist Paul or Peter or Carol or me to assist him. And if Bill weren't being called out, chances were that we were having company because Bill was forever bringing people home -- and Marion, bless her, always welcomed and fed them all. Often, beyond their names, we didn't know who these people were who were at the table with us. We had no idea why they were there or what their problems were. It didn't matter. We knew that they were in need.

"Peter's bedroom later was moved to the basement, into what had been the recreation room. Many mornings, Peter would awaken to find a stranger sleeping on the nearby sofa. During the night, Bill would have found someone who needed some place to stay. Sometimes, too, Bill and Marion would themselves

come out of their bedroom to find some unexpected person on the couch in the living room. Word was out that the door of 116 Rupert Street was never locked; anyone who needed warmth and shelter was welcome."

* * * * * * *

All this time, Marion's condition had been steadily worsening. Then, in 1966, there finally came terrible news: doctors informed Marion that she had "CMT" or "Charcot-Marie-Tooth Disease". (Medical specialists explained that their previous difficulty in making the diagnosis had probably been due to the fact that she had been so fine an athlete in her youth: her fine physical conditioning had masked or postponed some of the usual early symptoms.) Doctors had to explain to Marion and Bill that CMT is a dreadful sentence; the disorder is progressive and incurable. Slowly, the nervous system degenerates; sufferers lose normal use of their feet and legs, arms and hands. Muscles waste away. Victims find it difficult to walk; their balance becomes unstable. Their hands lose their coordination; simple tasks like holding a pen or handling cutlery are increasingly difficult. Pain and depression are constantly present. Eventually, total bed confinement is necessary with the patient being unable to take care of even the simplest functions of hygiene and grooming.

And so we see Bill, stretching himself ever thinner, serving others as though he is a professional counsellor, social worker, minister. While doing so, he is raising his own three young people and a niece whom he regards as a second daughter. He has a wife with a crippling and incurable neurological disease who will require more and more of his personal care And yet, while dealing with all this, his professional career is still his work in the business: there, he has to continue to pull his weight and meet all his responsibilities. It's becoming increasingly difficult for Bill to do all that he believes that God is calling him to do while at the same time fulfilling his obligations in the family firm. Something will have to give. Events in the fall of 1967 force a decision. By a strange coincidence, these events involve the same minister who four years earlier had assisted Bill to make his great "surrender".

CHAPTER FOUR

THE TURNING POINT

In 1966, the minister of St. Paul's United Church, Port Arthur, accepted a call to Knox-Metropolitan United Church in Regina[6]. He was asked to promote the same kind of renewal that had taken place in the Port Arthur congregation. He was 32 years of age. He had come close to exhausting himself at St. Paul's, but he accepted the new challenge with enthusiasm. At the time, Knox-Metropolitan was one of the largest United Church congregations in Western Canada with 2,700 members and a sanctuary that held 1,700. It had a proud history, having played a major role in church expansion across all Saskatchewan. By 1966, however, it was in the midst of a severe decline. Younger families were leaving in great numbers, moving to suburban churches; membership at worship was steadily dropping; the church building

---

[6] For American readers, it should be noted that Regina is located about 1,000 miles west of the Lakehead; it is the capital of the Province of Saskatchewan.

was greatly in need of restoration; the old pipe organ was on its last legs; most significantly, there were no spiritual cell groups within the congregation and there was no kind of evangelical outreach to the surrounding community.

With good intentions but also with the folly of his youth, the minister plunged into his new assignment, trying to replicate immediately the work that had been going on in Port Arthur. Evening services were started; morning services were broadcast; a second morning service was begun. A very large Casavant organ was purchased, and with that acquisition a vast ministry of music, involving five choirs, was initiated. Prayer groups and Bible study fellowships were established. Intensive pastoral visitation was instituted to cover all 1,000 families. Three new assistants were hired for the expanding youth programs.

For the first year, all seemed to go well. Church attendance dramatically increased; the Sunday School tripled in size. New programs for university students attracted more than 100 on Sunday nights.. A recorded "minute with God" telephone ministry received 600 to 700 calls each day. An outreach "coffee house" was established which attracted large numbers of young people. Two men volunteered as candidates for the ministry. Lives began to be "changed"; a 1967 Holy Week mission with a popular Toronto preacher brought many members into deeper discipleship. There was great enthusiasm across all sides of the congregation; things were proceeding smoothly.

Then unexpected difficulties arose: these centred on the installation of the new pipe organ and the renovation of the sanctuary. Preliminary architectural and engineering investigations revealed that one side of the old church had been slowly sinking into the prairie soil beneath it; to correct the problem, a major engineering project would be required. Then, too, it was discovered that the entire fabric of the building would need to be restored with new flooring, new wiring, the replacement of two furnaces, a re-leading of all the stained glass, and a repointing of much of the brickwork. These needs, and a multitude of other necessary changes, would carry with them a cost that was quite astronomical. A financial campaign organized to raise the necessary money failed dismally. Plans for the organ and the renovation were immediately put on hold; the dream of a remodelled and beautified church "fell through the cracks". The minister blamed himself for the problem.

"For a long time, probably from the moment of my ordination, the ministry had been my whole life. I had been obsessed with succeeding; and, of course, I had always been able to justify that

obsession by telling myself that it was all for the Kingdom of God. Yet that had been only partly true; I had also been pushing myself for the sake of having a successful 'career' in the church.

"In my drive to be the perfect minister, I set no limits. I worked 70 to 80 hours each week, never took a day off (literally), and used my annual holidays for other assignments in other churches. I conducted preaching missions wherever and whenever I was invited. I was driven by a fear of failure; I felt that everything was depending on me, that every sermon had to be better than the last, that every service had to see a larger congregation than the week before.

"I was so absorbed in my career that I neglected my wife and our three children. That neglect had been bad enough at St. Paul's; now, at Knox-Metropolitan, it became even more extreme. My family saw me only 'on the run'. Naturally, the marriage began to suffer. I had no time for my wife, but I couldn't see why she then began to have less and less time for me. We grew apart. I blamed her quite unfairly for the deterioration in our relationship. As the months went by, I became horribly, pathologically depressed.

"The failure of our financial campaign was my first major defeat in my ten years as a minister. I cannot describe how crushed I was as I saw our stewardship drive falling apart and going 'down the tubes': with it went my dream of a spectacular new sanctuary (to complement what I had come to regard as my 'spectacular' ministry). The failure confirmed my worst fears; it was proof to me that I was inadequate. I began questioning my calling, asking myself if there was any point continuing, wishing that I were in any other line of work but preaching. I became frightened, nervous, convinced that the fund-raising fiasco was but the harbinger of much greater failures. Soon, I found myself unable to eat or sleep. I felt isolated; no one seemed able to understand. To the contrary: everyone still kept telling me how marvellous a job I was doing. I felt trapped.

"At this point, I met a very beautiful young woman who was separated from an abusive husband; she was raising her five children on her own. She telephoned the church at a time of special need. I was able to help, and she thereafter regarded me as a 'knight in shining armour'. She was always a light-hearted, happy, kindly person; and, whenever I was with her, all my cares seem to vanish. She made me believe in myself again. In her company, I began to feel that life was again worth living. The attraction she held for me soon became an unbreakable addiction.

"I was aware of the impossible situation in which I was placing myself; but, by then, the physical and nervous strains of the previous ten years were taking over. Without realizing it, I was into the midst of a physical and emotional breakdown. My weight dropped to 109 pounds. Friends told me that I looked like a man twice my age. I passed most of my work over to my assistants and locked myself away in my office for much of each day. When I preached, I felt like the hypocrite I was; I could not bring myself to conduct the sacraments. No one knew what was wrong, and I knew that I dared tell no one. I, myself, didn't know how very sick I was.

"One sunny morning in late October '67, I decided that the only way to escape the pain and turmoil was to kill myself and that the most effective way to do that would be to jump from the eight-storey bell tower of Knox-Metropolitan. I climbed to the tower platform. I removed one of the screens and sat on the ledge, dropping pebbles to hear them click on the street below, timing their fall, trying to screw up the courage to leap out into space.

"For some reason, I decided that I should return to my office to empty my pockets and write a note of explanation. While down in the office, some impulse led me to call Bill Crooks in Port Arthur; it was about 1 p.m. in Ontario, and Bill was at work in his office in the pharmacy. He was surprised to hear from me, but I couldn't bring myself to explain to him why I was calling. (I, myself, didn't understand why I had wanted to speak with him.) I didn't share with Bill any of the trouble I was in, and I assured him that there was nothing of importance to report. After a few moments, I said goodbye and hung up the 'phone.

"Bill, however, was not buying my story. Immediately, he called me back and kept me on the telephone for more than twenty minutes as he described all the good work that was still continuing within the St. Paul's congregation. When at last I hung up the receiver, I found that the mad impulse to kill myself had left me. I felt exhausted. I drove home, lay down across a bed, and fell asleep.

"At 8 p.m., I was awakened by the ringing of the doorbell. It was Bill Crooks, suitcase in hand. As soon as our 'phone call had ended, he had sensed that he had to go to Regina. He had raced to the airport and had caught the next flight westward. (To be honest, I was not at all pleased to see him. Here was one more person to complicate that hopeless mess into which I had fallen.)

"In the days that followed, Bill stuck with me 'closer than a brother'. He knew that something was destroying me. He didn't pester me to tell him what it was. He simply stayed with me, inventing excuses to come with me wherever I went. Four nights later, following the Sunday evening service, the two of us went for a long walk along the darkened streets of Regina. Bit by bit, I blurted out the terrible truths: I wanted out of the ministry; I didn't know what to do about my marriage; I was torn between two women; I was in a situation from which I could not break free.

"At that moment, had Bill decided to moralise and lecture, he could easily have destroyed me with a tongue-lashing. He could have told me what I already knew only too well -- that I was a pathetic excuse for a human being, that I was a hypocrite, that I was behaving like an idiot, that I was failing all the people who had ever put their faith in my ministry, that I was betraying the Church and turning my back on God. Bill could easily have driven me back into my suicidal despair.

"Instead, Bill simply said, 'I've seen this coming for a long time. Even back in Port Arthur, I knew that you and your marriage were coming apart. I'd really like to meet this new person in your life.' A great burden rolled off me: here was someone who knew the worst about me and yet who didn't hate me.

"Bill's subsequent meetings with my special friend were remarkable. She, too, was desperately needing someone in whom she could confide about the impossible situation in which we found ourselves. In one of these private counselling sessions with Bill, she gave her life to Christ and turned our dilemma over to Him. Her Christian commitment was to bring an entirely new dimension into our relationship; henceforth, whatever would happen between the two of us would be in God's hands, not mine.

"When Bill flew back to Port Arthur two days later, he left me with hope, hope that my situation could be resolved, hope that some good could come out of the mess I had made of things, hope that God would straighten out my life. Thoughts of suicide had been shelved.

"Bill had been a week with me, a full week away from Marion and children, a full week away from his work in the family business."

Bill's visit to the minister in Regina marked an end and a beginning, an end and a beginning both in his life and in the minister's. Because of the visit, the minister was given the courage to seek medical help. Doctors quickly diagnosed that he was "burned out", was suffering from mental and emotional exhaustion, and was in the midst of a major nervous collapse. He agreed to enter the psychiatric ward of the Winnipeg General Hospital. There, he resigned from his pastorate at Knox-Metropolitan. His wife, devastated by the circumstances of losing her home and her marriage, had to begin to pack the family belongings, preparing to leave the Regina manse for a new home two thousand miles away to be where she could be near her family. During these weeks of stress and turmoil, Bill made four more flying trips to Regina, trying to assist her, hoping to bring some healing, understanding, and forgiveness into the difficult situation.

Bill's four trips to Regina, like the original trip, were all at his own expense and on his company's time. In the midst of them, his old ulcer problems returned; he had to go to the Mayo Clinic for diagnosis and treatment. Bill's family and friends naturally began to question his priorities. With Marion's failing health, with his children needing him at home, why was he always so involved with the problems of other families? Why not with his own?   Naturally, too, his brothers, his partners in business, believed that he was losing his perspective: Bill was being paid to work for the company, not to give counsel a thousand miles away. How could he expect the family firm to cover his absences?   Bill felt the tension that was all around him: where did his duty lie?

The tension increased when Bill took the minister from the Winnipeg hospital into his own home. Bill and Marion found that that decision brought even greater trouble to them.   Again, the minister takes up the tale.

"After two weeks in Winnipeg, I was discharged. The doctors had found nothing wrong except total exhaustion. I had had a major nervous breakdown, I was told. It would be many months before I would be strong enough again to work -- and, even then, where would a broken and disgraced minister find a job?

"A more immediate problem lay before me: where was I to go? It was impossible for me to return to the home that was disintegrating in Regina: my wife sent word that I would not be welcome there. My mother in far-off Ottawa, already with a chronic heart condition, had worried herself into a heart attack over me and was in the hospital. My father had then had a coronary, himself, and had died. My older brother and his wife disowned me in disgust, vowing that they would never again speak to me. My ministerial colleagues were equally distant and judgmental; they had previously been suspicious of my work, and now I had handed them proof that an evangelical ministry was of dubious value. My employer, the United Church of Canada, chose to ignore the whole situation and offered no advice or assistance; in the Church's eyes, I had ceased to exist. If ever a man felt utterly on his own, it was I.

"Hearing of my dilemma, Bill and Marion telephoned the hospital, inviting me to make my home with them. And so, on

December 19th, 1967, I crept back to Port Arthur. Eighteen months previously, I had left that city, loved and admired by many; now I was a broken man, without possessions or prospects of any work, without family and almost without friends.

"I don't think that Bill was prepared for the reception I received or for the criticism that was levelled at him for his having assisted me. It was made painfully clear that I was a pariah and had had no business returning to Port Arthur. Gossip, much of it false, swirled around me. Anyone who tried to help me was ostracised. The Church, at least in 1968, wasn't ready to accept a 'lost shepherd'. Anyone who stood by me was considered an enemy of the 'establishment'.

"Among my few supporters and friends, Bill and Marion suffered most; they bore the brunt of the criticism. Why in God's Name were they making themselves a part of my scandal? Why were they bringing embarrassment to my successor at St. Paul's? Why were they creating controversy for the Crooks' family name? And why was Bill continuing to go out on a limb for me? (Bill was still defending me, still doing everything he could to help me deal with my desperate situation.)

"Despite all the criticism levelled at him, Bill continued in his limitless service for me. Knowing my anguish and concern for my three little children, Bill made at his own expense two more costly trips to visit my daughters and my son, this time in their new home, simply to be able to assure me that they were coping well in their setting now so far away."

In all this, without having to be told, Bill and Marion realized that a choice had to made. Bill could not continue to run a full-time "counsel-and-rescue" service while attempting to hold down a full-time position in the family company. There was no doubt where Bill's heart lay -- or his gifts: so many lives had already been changed by his work and witness. After weeks of prayer and discussion, the decision came. He would leave the pharmacy and would trust God to guide him into a new work.

Bill's departure from J. W. Crooks and Company was completely amicable. His brothers thanked him for his years of work with them. He was given his full share of the value of the family business. Then, like Abraham, Bill turned his back on all the security he had known and went forth in obedience to his God, "not knowing where he was to go."

CHAPTER FIVE

"WOUNDED TO SERVE"

With Bill's decision to make counselling a full-time profession, his life began quickly to change. Many of the experiences which were now to come to him were things which he and Marion had been able to foresee; while these would sometimes be difficult to bear, they would not come as shocks. Other experiences, however, would be totally unexpected, painful, and devastating; for these Bill and Marion could have made no preparation; their only defence would be their absolute trust in the God they had met in Jesus Christ. That defence was to prove solid and secure: without anger towards God and without despair over their lot, the Crooks were to meet the smashing blows which life now was to level at them. Those who watched could only marvel! Only a Higher Power could give Bill and Marion the courage, wisdom, and grace to triumph over events that would have destroyed most people.

From the Scriptures, the Crooks knew that Jesus had promised His followers no easy road; to the contrary, He had warned those who wished to come after Him that His was a narrow and difficult way; inevitably, discipleship would involve suffering. There could be no Kingdom without a cross. His cross stood before Him; so, too, a cross would stand before all who walked His way.

Why suffering should always be so central in the spiritual life is a question which from the beginning has taxed theologians and philosophers. Why are those who seek only God's best so often assailed by the worst life has to offer? Why do terrible things happen to those who least deserve them? Many answers have been given; the wisest, perhaps, comes from St. Paul. Following his conversion to Christianity, Paul had found that his life was filled with a series of difficulties and catastrophes. Paul's response to this? "I am content with weaknesses. insults, hardships, persecutions, and calamities -- for I have learned that it is when I am weak that I am truly strong." "I am content with my sufferings because, through my sufferings, God is enabled to accomplish things which otherwise would be impossible. I know that in all things God is at work for good with those who love him."

Thornton Wilder writes, "In love's army, only the wounded can serve." Only those who themselves suffer in life are equipped to minister to a suffering world. If that is so, then, perhaps, it explains why God allowed the Crooks to endure so much. Certainly it would explain why they were able to serve so effectively. As we shall now see, not long after Bill had given himself to his new mission, he and Marion were deeply wounded. As we continue with their story, who can doubt that it was precisely because they were so battered and hurt that they then were so effective in sharing God's love with others? They had been "wounded to serve."

* * * * * * *

When he left the family business, the most urgent and immediate problem Bill faced was the practical matter of money. How was he now to support Marion and his children? His decision to become a counsellor meant real monetary sacrifice: never again would he have the income and financial security he had to that point enjoyed. He was now without a job, and there was no guarantee where or when he would find one. He had no other source of income. Still, of course he had that generous settlement from his share in the Crooks' pharmaceutical business -- or did he? Did Bill find that this large "nest egg" of security was also required of him as part of the cost of his discipleship? It seems that that, indeed, was the case. He appears to have lost everything in order to help someone in need.

In August, 1997, as plans were being made for Bill's memorial service in Thunder Bay, Jamie, his older brother, mentioned the settlement that Bill had received thirty years earlier. "You know," he said, "it's a strange thing about that money! It was a handsome sum, but Bill seems to have given most of it away almost as soon as he received it. He absolutely refused ever to discuss with us what he had done with it. We think that he co-signed some sort of loan that went bad. Bill would never tell anyone what happened. I doubt that even Marion ever knew."

In the weeks following that memorial service, that story was repeated among Bill's circle of friends; and, as this book was being prepared, one of Bill's friends stepped forward to provide this probable explanation:

"I'm in a position of responsibility, and so I don't wish to identify myself; even after all these years, there could be repercussions. Yet I feel a real need to confess. Having recently heard about the 'disappearance' of Bill's inheritance, I feel that I can probably shed light on it. I very much fear that I am the person responsible for his loss.

"Back in 1967, despite the fact the I was a married man, I had a 'summer romance' with one of the junior officers in our

company. For me, it was nothing serious; we never became deeply involved. I regarded it as little more than a mild flirtation. For her, however, it had greater significance. She was unhappily married to a man who was one of the shadier characters in Northwestern Ontario, someone who was 'rough and tough'; he was extremely abusive to her.

"Although our foolish 'fling' soon ended (and ended completely), the experience had convinced my friend that she had had enough of her marriage. She told her husband that she wanted a legal separation. In the bitter arguments that followed, he wormed it out of her that she had had a 'crush' on me. At that, he became enraged, threatening to go to our company president to demand that both she and I be fired. He said that he was going to sue me for 'alienation of affection'. He was going to destroy my marriage and my reputation. I was in a panic. I feared that he would do irreparable harm.

"I knew Bill from our work together at the Y. And I knew that Bill had had some contact with this man who was so angry with me, and so I sought his advice. Bill told me not to worry and said that he would deal with the situation. And he did! Within a week or so, all the harassing 'phone calls had stopped. The threats had been withdrawn. Peace had been restored. I asked Bill what had happened and was told in effect, 'It's none of your business. Don't worry about it! It's over and done with! Forget it!'

"A long, long time later, I had coffee with the woman in question (who had since divorced her husband and had moved to another city.) We reminisced about that strange summer when we had been special friends to one another. I wondered what Bill had done to cast oil upon the troubled waters. She seemed surprised: 'Don't you know? My husband ran up another of his huge gambling debts, and Bill co-signed a loan for the repayment on condition that he back off completely from bothering you. Don't worry,' she said as she saw the expression on my face, 'I'm sure that it was paid.'

"Now, however, I fear that that debt wasn't paid. Now that I have learned about the disappearance of Bill's inheritance, I am sure that Bill was left 'holding the bag' for me. I believe that he risked and lost his inheritance in order to protect me from a bully -- (and from the consequences of my own stupidity.) That someone would do this for a friend

is amazing! Even more amazing is that Bill would do this and never embarrass me by telling me about it! He never let me know what helping me had cost him! For my sake, he took that secret to his grave."

Thus, we see that, even as Bill walked away from the security of his position in the family firm, he also walked away from the security provided by his inheritance, surrendering it "in the service of love", being prepared to lose everything in order to meet another's need. This way of total commitment had been Bill's way ever since that afternoon in 1963 when he had given his life to Christ; he was to continue in that way for the remainder of his life.

* * * * * * *

After several months of searching, Bill found a position as a counsellor on the staff of the newly formed Addiction Rehabilitation Unit, (later to be known as the Smith Clinic), in St. Joseph's Hospital in Port Arthur. His personal knowledge of Twelve Step programs, his own experience with addictive substances, and his natural empathy with people who suffer made him an ideal person for such a position. He soon found, however, that the work had many frustrations. Several of the psychiatrists dealing with patients either did not understand or did not sympathize with the Twelve Step approach to recovery Their misguided answer to alcoholism was to take men and women off alcohol by substituting other mood-altering drugs; one addiction was being traded for others. Bill was discouraged because he knew that there was a better answer.

****

Sister Sharon Miller worked with Bill on the same unit and was impressed by his special gifts as a helper and healer. She writes about a revealing conversation she had at this time.

> "It was early in Bill's time with us on Three South in St. Joseph's Hospital. Three South had formerly been the Obstetrical Unit of the hospital, a place for new life to be fostered. It had recently been designated as the Addiction Rehabilitation Unit, (later to be known as the Smith Clinic) -- still a place for the fostering of new life
>
> "Bill Crooks came to share a cup of tea with me. I recall asking him with a smile, 'What do you want to be when you grow up?' He pointed to our director's office and said, 'I want to sit at that man's desk.' 'And, Bill, what does your God want you to be?' After a pause, he responded with

conviction, 'I believe He also wants me to sit at that desk.'

"That night I gave Bill the address for the Hazelden Foundation in Minnesota. One year later, soon after completing his Counsellor Training Program, Bill returned to Three South and, indeed, some years later, took over the director's desk. From that centre, from that desk, Bill was to share his spiritual journey through the Twelve Steps with so many others."

With Sister Sharon's pointing him towards Hazelden, Bill realized that new sacrifices were now being demanded of him and Marion. Bill knew that Sister Sharon was right: if he were to advance in his new career, professional training would be necessary and the best place to take such training was at Hazelden[7] in Centre City, Minnesota (near Minneapolis). He knew that to study at Hazelden would be difficult for him, difficult in terms of family separation, difficult in terms of family finances. Marion was now experiencing more of the symptoms of CMT. Her balance was insecure; her walking was clumsy; with her illness, she was suffering from deep depression. Bill would have to leave her.

---

[7] Hazelden is a training and treatment centre, famous around the world for its work in the field of addiction and dependency diseases.

Moreover, he would have to take a leave of absence from St. Joseph's Hospital and be without salary for a full year. Of financial necessity, the beautiful house on Rupert Street would soon have to be exchanged for a much more modest place in a humbler section of the city. No less painful would be the need to sell the cottage on Hawkeye Lake, that spot which had been the centre of the Crooks' summers for so many years -- another real sacrifice which Bill and Marion accepted without complaint or self-pity.

Believing that he was following God's guidance, Bill moved to Hazelden. He and Marion saw each other once or twice a month. She sometimes flew to Minneapolis; more often, Bill drove home, a 400-mile journey that can be tiresome and very hazardous in winter weather. (During this year, Bill had a remarkable escape from death. One morning, after a lecture at Hazelden, he went to the parking lot to start his car. As soon as he turned the key, he sensed that something was wrong. He threw open the door and rolled out onto the ground; in that same instant, the automobile exploded into a fireball. Had his response been one second slower, Bill would have been engulfed in the flames.)

A former priest, a man who later was to become a close friend and colleague of Bill Crooks, tells of coming to know Bill at this time:

"I first heard about Bill Crooks in 1969 when I, myself, was in recovery in the after care program of the Addiction Rehabilitation Unit at St. Joseph's Hospital in Port Arthur. While I was there, my superiors determined that I should go into Clinical Pastoral Education at Hazelden. I was told by the staff at St. Joseph's that I would there meet Bill who was at Hazelden as a counsellor-in-training. Everyone had great praise for him, and all were looking forward to his return to the Smith Clinic.

"At Hazelden, I came to admire Bill very much. I attended his lectures, worked in his therapy group, and attended A.A. meetings with him. He was wholeheartedly committed to the program; he fully lived the Twelve Steps.

"I didn't know at the time that I would later be privileged to work with Bill when he began a new clinic, the Eppley Centre, in Omaha, Nebraska. There, with him, I would establish A.A. groups and facilitate workshops and retreats. There, too, I would witness how miraculously he dealt with those heavy blows that life brought him in the deaths of his children and in Marion's terrible illness.

"Bill succeeded in all he did because he admitted the absolute powerlessness and total unmanageability of his life. He knew beyond any question that, in and of himself, he could do nothing. He had completely turned his life over to the care of his Higher Power and in everything he did he acted with absolute faith in his Higher Power. And his Higher Power never failed him."

* * * * * * *

Following the completion of his year at Hazelden, Bill returned to his family and to his work at the Smith. Marion's health was continuing to decline; walking up or down stairs had become impossible. She had started to use leg braces and a cane. For Bill, the frustrations of the work at the Smith Clinic were still present. He was certain that many of the medical staff were taking approaches that were counter-productive to their patients' recovery. His hands, however, were tied; he could not prevent physicians and psychiatrists from prescribing more drugs for people who already were chemically dependent. Eventually, Bill left the Smith Clinic and moved across Thunder Bay to Fort William to become the local director of the Ontario Addiction Research Foundation; however, this new work provided other sorts of frustrations. Applying for grants, organizing publicity, setting up educational programs -- these all were worthy endeavours but they didn't give Bill much opportunity to use his greatest gift, that of personally reaching people who needed God's healing love.

* * * * * * *

Then, on January 16th, 1971, Bill and Marion received a crushing blow. Their younger son, Paul, 17 years old, a young man with a winning personality and with fine athletic skills, had gone on a weekend holiday to Lutsen, a resort across the American border, about fifty miles south of the Lakehead. Paul was a good swimmer; and, one night, after he and his friends had been in the pool, as the others were leaving for their rooms, he took one final dive. Something went wrong; on the way down, his head slammed into the board. He was fatally injured; he died within an hour at a hospital in the nearby town of Grand Marais.

Peter, the older brother, writes about that night:

"The night Paul died, I was out with friends at a ski party. I arrived home quite late to find my parents about to leave for the hospital at Grand Marais, near Lutsen. They knew only that Paul had been hurt in a swimming accident at the Lutsen Resort. We drove together to

Grand Marais; I dozed in the back seat, thinking that Paul's injury was surely not too serious. When we arrived at the hospital, we were stunned to learn that Paul was dead. Much of what happened thereafter is a blank in my memory, but I remember that Dad seemed to be at peace with the tragedy. He wasn't angry as he might have been expected to be. He didn't blame anyone, not Paul's friends, not the resort. Nor did he blame God..."

A family friend writes about Bill and Marion in their immense grief:

"I had seen the Crooks reach out to so many others who were in trouble: they had been able to give so much comfort and hope to those in dark places. I wondered how they now would handle this tragedy which had come to them. I should have known. There were tears but there was no self-pity. They were more concerned about how others were managing than they were concerned for themselves. They planned a funeral service that was positive: the emphasis was not on the brevity of Paul's life but on the goals he had achieved, not on their sorrows as a family but on the new life Paul was now beginning. Later, at the graveside service, the clouds parted; the

winter sun shone down on Bill's face. I don't think I have ever seen anyone so much at peace."

Whatever the peace that Bill and Marion were given, they still had experienced a great shock -- (there can be none greater than the unexpected death of a child) -- and shock hurries the progression of CMT. Those nearest Marion soon noticed a further deterioration in her condition.

* * * * * * *

Shortly after Paul's death, Bill was handed an unexpected challenge: he was invited to become the founder and director of the Eppley Centre in Omaha, a new drug and alcohol treatment centre which was to be connected with the Nebraska Methodist Hospital in that city. Despite the magnificent opportunities it presented, the invitation was not an easy one to accept. Moving to Omaha would mean other sacrifices. Bill and Marion loved Thunder Bay[8] ; there, they were surrounded by friends and family. Bill's brothers were all nearby, as was his elderly mother with whom he was very close. Peter would have to be left behind; Carol, too, was at an age where she would not choose to be uprooted. Still, the opportunity had come to do what Bill had long believed God had called him to do -- to direct his

---
[8] By this time, Port Arthur and Fort William had been amalgamated into the City of Thunder Bay.

own treatment program. With much sorrow, the Crooks said farewell to Thunder Bay and to the friendships and way of life they had known.

Bill, Marion, and Carol went together to Omaha. There, after seeing her parents settled into their new home, Carol returned to Thunder Bay to work in the pharmacy and share an apartment with Peter. The Crooks busied themselves in their new surroundings. Bill faced an immense amount of work in founding and organizing the new clinic, recruiting staff, coordinating his work with other state and city agencies, and making the public aware that this new facility was available; (prior to this time, the nearest treatment centre for alcoholics and addicts had been at Hazelden, in far-off Minnesota.) Bill spoke to service clubs and in churches; he was interviewed on television and radio; he addressed doctors' conferences and health associations; he wrote articles for the newspapers. And always he had the care of Marion who was increasingly dependent on him.

At this stage, Marion wrote the minister-friend whom Bill had rescued from his disastrous situation in Regina. It is a remarkable letter from a woman who was victim of an incurable disease, a woman who only six months earlier had lost her younger son. It reveals the degree to which she and Bill were relying solely on God for guidance and strength. She wrote,

"I know that you keep telling people that everything is okay with you, but I feel compelled to write to you. When I go to bed, I often can't sleep because of my concern for you.

"Dear friend, God has given you a second chance at life. I'm afraid, however, that you are now regarding your life, not as a gift, but as a kind of penance. I don't think that you are enjoying it as you should, and I don't believe you are really being grateful for all that God has given you and is still giving you.

"You must know and believe that God wants you to be happy. He wants you to enjoy the abundant life He has promised. You have been completely and totally forgiven for the past: the only unforgivable sin is to refuse to accept the forgiveness which God extends to us in Christ.

"Keep things simple. Quit looking at the past. Live every day knowing that it is the first day of the rest of your life and could possibly be the last day of your life.

"I know that you miss your children terribly, but so do we miss our kids when we're down here. But you really haven't lost them, even as we haven't really lost ours -- even our Paul isn't really lost to us! You don't know what the future will bring you, but you're not to concern yourself with it. That's God's business, not yours.

"Today is our silver wedding anniversary, and I can honestly say that Bill and I have never known such happiness as we have at this time. Remember: if it weren't for your ministry, we might never have had this wonderful life. Bill especially will be eternally grateful for the way God used you to help him find the way."

* * * * * * *

Only six months after that letter was written, the Crooks were dealt another stunning blow! On the evening of November 24th, 1972, Carol's car was in a Thunder Bay garage for repairs. She and a girl friend had been out to a concert and, on their way home, had missed a bus. The night was bitterly cold, and the wind was freezing. The girls decided to hitchhike; (ironically, this was the first time that Carol had ever hitchhiked.) A new sports car pulled up, and they got in. The automobile sped away. Carol and her friend realized at once that the driver was drunk, but it was too late. Wanting to impress his passengers with the power of his new vehicle, the driver put the accelerator to the floor. The car spun out of control and smashed into a telephone pole. Carol died in the hospital a few hours later. She was only eighteen.

Friends describe how, in this tragedy, Bill and Marion used their faith to inspire others and to prove that St. Paul was right when he said, "In everything that happens to us, we know that God is at work for good with those who love Him . . ."

"With a group of friends, I went to the airport to meet the flight from Omaha. We didn't know what we were going to be able to say or do for Bill and Marion. How could we greet these dear souls who had lost two children within the space twenty-one months? We, ourselves, were in shock and tears.

"Marion came through the door, bravely smiling. Obviously, she had been crying; but she brushed the tears away and embraced each one of us. Bill was calm, serene, deeply at peace. He saw me crying and came to me and enfolded me in his arms. As I continued sobbing, he took a half-step back and looked into my eyes. 'It's okay,' he whispered, 'it's all okay.'

> "We had come to the airport to comfort them; instead, they were comforting us."

Or this amazing story:

> "I had flown from Toronto to be with Bill and Marion whose friendship and Christian witness had meant so much to me. As soon as I arrived in Thunder Bay, I wanted to see Bill but was told that he would be unavailable for a few hours. I asked where he was and was told that he had gone to spend time at the jail with the man who had killed his daughter. I don't know what Bill said to that man, but I know that he went there because he wanted both to help him and to help himself. He didn't want anger or bitterness to have control.

Or this:

> "I have never seen so powerful a testimony to God's power and love as I saw in Bill and Marion at the time of Carol's death. They were both so strong and loving; there was no sense that they were gritting their teeth and forcing themselves to put on a brave front. They were lifting their sorrow into the hands of God. As I looked at the expression on Bill's face, I thought of the cry of Job: 'Even though God should slay me, yet will

I trust Him!'"

Or this:

"Following the interment service, a number of us went to be with Bill and Marion at the house of one of Bill's brothers. As is usual on such occasions, we had refreshments and chatted with one another about various things that were taking place in the city. At one point, someone in the room mentioned that Bob, one of Bill's former patients at the Smith Clinic, was about to lose his business because he had not been able to handle his mortgage; $ 18,000 was overdue.

"A little later, I saw Bill putting on his overcoat. He told me that he needed some fresh air and wanted to go for a walk. And, no, he didn't want any company. He was gone for about three hours and then returned, took off his coat, and rejoined the group. He said nothing about where he had been, and I thought no more about it.

"Some years later, I heard that Bob had not lost his business after all. It turns out that that afternoon, Bill had walked down to St. Paul's United Church, had gone into the chapel, and had prayed,

'Lord, my friend, Bob, needs money for his mortgage. Where can I get it for him?' Names had come to him and, from the church office, Bill had made 'phone calls. The whole sum had been guaranteed that afternoon.

"To go out to raise money for a former patient on the same afternoon in which you've laid your only daughter in her grave, that's something superhuman, supernatural! Only God could enable someone to do that! And Bill never said a word about it to anyone. I don't know if even Bob ever learned how his debt had been paid."

****

Following the funeral, Bill and Marion soon returned to Omaha and to his work at the Eppley Centre. Again, the shock of Carol's death had accelerated the progress of Marion's illness. She became less able to move without falling; her cane was now replaced by a walker. She was in constant pain, yet she never complained. As much as was possible, she continue to follow a normal routine, and always she had a warm smile and words of encouragement for anyone else who was in difficulty. When people knew through what dark waters she was passing, her message of God's unfailing love held special power. So, too, with Bill at the Eppley Centre. The blows that had fallen on him, far from shaking his faith. had only increased it. They had brought even greater power and conviction to his message. One medical doctor who went to Eppley for treatment at about this time tells of his first encounter with Bill.

> "Bill gave one of the first lectures I had at Eppley. He stood up there at the front of the room, and talked and talked about living your life by handing it all over to God and trusting Him completely, and I'm there, saying to myself the whole time, "Baloney, baloney, baloney!"
>
> "But Bill was an impressive guy. Later, he went on to speak of his own trust in God. 'Within the last two years, I've lost both a son and daughter in accidents,' he told us. I took a second look at the man. Maybe he did have something to teach me after all.
>
> "As time passed, I discovered that Bill was the most inspiring and most spiritually-oriented man I had ever met. He had the ability to get people to climb out of the rut of their 'stinking thinking' and hand over their whole lives, the good, the bad, and the ugly, to the care of God.
>
> "How did he do this? Well, looking back, I realize that the thing that made Bill so convincing for me and for a lot of others

was the fact that he had endured so much and yet was able still to live so great a life! Bill kept on telling us that we, too, could trust God's goodness with all our trials and problems. God would never fail us.

"Had Bill had a 'cushy' or comfortable life, we could have brushed his words away. 'Oh sure, sure! Easy for you to say! You don't know what it's like.' But when we knew that this man had faced the worst that life could bring, the death of his children, his wife's incurable illness, and a tough, tough job, and still he was believing that God is loving and that life is good, then we had to admit that he had an answer to life that we had been missing!"

And so, through the many sacrifices that he made to equip himself for service and through those great unexpected "woundings" which had struck both him and Marion, Bill learned that God was preparing him for special service. Like St. Paul, he could now declare from his own experience, "I am content with all that has befallen me -- for I have learned that it is when I am weak that I am truly strong. And I know this: that in everything that has happened, God has been at work within my life to bring forth good. We are more than conquerors through Him who loved us.

I am convinced that neither life nor death . . . nor anything else in all creation can separate us from the love of God which is in Christ Jesus our Lord."

As one reads the stories in the chapters that follow, who can doubt that it was because Bill had been so "wounded" -- that it was because of the disciplines he had accepted and the sorrows he had endured -- that it was because he had lost a beloved son and daughter -- that it was because he was daily seeing his life partner dying before his eyes -- that it was because he had again and again been driven to his knees in prayer -- that it was because he had experienced all this and more that he was so able to minister to those shattered lives which God brought to him for healing? Bill could meet them in their pain for he, too, had been wounded, "wounded to serve . . ."

CHAPTER SIX

HEALING SHATTERED LIVES

All the time that Bill had been dealing with his grief over the deaths of Paul and Carol and coping with his concerns for Marion in her illness, his work in the new treatment centre had continued without a break. Indeed, the work had been steadily growing. When he had founded the Eppley Centre, it had had thirty beds; within a year, it had thirty-eight beds; within the next year it had sixty beds; within another two years, it had eighty-two beds. Asked to explain the steady growth, Bill took no credit. "It's the impact of our 'graduates'," he told a reporter. "People are seeing that recovery is possible. They meet a friend who has been in his cups for twenty-five years and discover that he's now been freed from his compulsion to drink; they begin to wonder if they, too, could be helped; and they come to us."

Bill was among the first to advocate active intervention in the disease of dependency. He decried the belief that family and friends have to wait until the alcoholic or the addict has "hit bottom" and has realized for himself his desperate situation; Bill pioneered the technique of staging "interventions" to confront the sick person with clear evidence of what he was doing to himself and to others. More often than not, these encounters would take the "tough love approach", but Bill insisted that with alcoholism drastic measures were needed. "This is an issue of life and death," he declared. "There is no time to wait for the alcoholic to ask for help; he or she may never live that long."

In Omaha, Bill also launched a special program for 'teenage addicts and alcoholics. He noted that less than fifty percent of the younger people who went through treatment were remaining sober, and he was convinced that this was because little after-treatment was available. From the Eppley Centre, 'teens were being returned to the same homes and neighbourhoods in which they had become sick. He spoke about the problem at service clubs, church meetings, medical conferences, and on radio and television. At his urging, the Kiewit Foundation of Omaha gave a million dollar grant for the establishment of "Methodist Midtown", two halfway houses for 'teens. All the places in this new facility were taken even before it was opened; in fact, by the time it was opened, there was a six-month waiting list for girls and an eight-month list for boys! "Methodist Midtown" proved its worth immediately. The rate of permanent recovery rose from fifty to seventy-five percent.

The successes at Eppley aroused interest, not only in Omaha, but across Nebraska and beyond. Increasingly, Bill was invited to speak about his work at conferences and conventions, often to audiences with scores of medical specialists, psychiatrists, clergy, and civic and state officials in the audiences. To those who had known the Bill Crooks of earlier years, this fact was remarkable because Bill had formerly been very insecure in any attempts he had made at public speaking. When, for example, he had had to make a few comments at the opening of a new swimming pool at the "Y" in Port Arthur, he had found the experience excruciatingly difficult; he had described his brief speech to a friend as "the worst thing I've ever had to do." Now, however, he was speaking everywhere, and speaking confidently and convincingly. An interviewer asked him about this: after all, he didn't even have a high school diploma and, apart from that year at Hazelden, had had no academic training. How did he have the authority to speak to audiences made up of professionals in the field? Bill's response would be no surprise to those who knew him:

"I simply turn it over to God and ask Him what I should say. I know that on my own I am way beyond my depth. I ask

God to use me and to tell me what the messages should be. It's exactly the same as when I speak with individuals. When I have to deal with a man or woman who has a problem, much of the time I have no idea what he or she should do. Only God knows. I ask Him to let me know. And God does -- provided that I am willing to get out of the way and listen."

* * * * * * *

As word of the work at Eppley continued to spread, Bill received invitations to move to other cities to establish treatment programs. Over all these contacts, Bill and Marion prayed, asking God what He would have them do; and always the invitations were rejected. Then, in 1976, a request came from the Mississippi Baptist Hospital in Jackson: there was an urgent need to establish a chemical dependency unit in that city. At the time, in all the "Deep South", the only such treatment centre was in North Carolina. Would Bill come and do in Mississippi what he had done in Nebraska? Bill and Marion prayed long about this invitation. Jackson was even further from Thunder Bay. Marion's health was declining; within a few years, she would be entirely confined to bed. The work in Omaha was running smoothly; Bill now had a well-trained staff working with him; and he and Marion had made many deep friendships in that city. But God said, "Go." And the Crooks said, "Yes."

Bill's work at Jackson became largely a repetition and extension of his work in Omaha. The unit began with 32 beds and then soon doubled and eventually tripled in size. A new team of counsellors was recruited. After-treatment programs were established Physicians and psychiatrists in the hospital were persuaded (sometimes with difficulty) that prescription drugs were not the answer to alcoholism and addiction. A satellite centre was then established in Columbus with Bill travelling back and forth while also providing direction from Jackson. By now, Bill had become recognized as an authority on treatment and recovery; from all across the South, there came requests for speeches, lectures, interviews. And as the months and years went by, the miracles of Omaha were repeated in Jackson; lives were changed, and hundreds of men and women had their fatal illness arrested. And always, Bill gave God all the credit: he insisted that what was happening was entirely God's doing, not his.

* * * * * * *

Earlier in this book, we read the stories of some of Bill's friends whom he helped to recovery in those years before he became a professional in the field of dependency. Here now are the stories are the stories told by some of the people whose shattered lives were healed in Bill's clinics in Omaha and Jackson.

****

Some speak of the unexpected love which they found in Bill. Here is one man's account of his first meeting with Bill:

"I was sent 'kicking and screaming' from Thunder Bay to have treatment in Omaha. I didn't want help although I knew I needed it. I had no choice about going to Omaha. My family and my employer issued an ultimatum, and so I complied -- but I was there in a most miserable and obstinate frame of mind. I was determined that my life was not going to be changed. I would handle my problems in my own way.

"The counsellor to whom I had been assigned must have torn out his hair. Step One, the admission that I was powerless over alcohol and that my life was unmanageable, I absolutely refused to take. The problem was not simply that I was being stubborn; I was incapable of taking that step. I couldn't admit, even to myself, that I was beaten. And without Step One, I couldn't proceed with the program.

"After using on me every counselling technique known to man, my counsellor began to threaten me with the fact that, since all else had failed, he would have to send me to see Bill Crooks. I had heard about Bill from some of the other patients. The consensus was that he was a 'tough cookie' who would stand no fooling around. I was assured that having a session with him would be a miserable experience.

"There came the day when I was told to report to Mr. Crooks. I was honestly afraid as I walked up the stairs to his office. I thought that he would scold me or bully me or threaten to expel me from the clinic.

"When I entered his office, I was surprised to meet this quiet, friendly, nice-looking grey-haired man who smiled at me and asked me to have a seat. He then walked around his desk, pulled up another chair, and sat squarely in front of me, so close to me that our knees were almost touching. He looked me in the eye, and then he began to talk to me.

"He didn't talk about me at all. He told me about himself. He told me about the kind of man he had been before he had given his life to God. He didn't hold anything back. He was very open as he described what alcohol had done to him in earlier years. He told me about the new way of life he had found with God. He told me that he had been absolutely powerless and then described what had happened when he had allowed God to take control. And he ended by saying that he was truly concerned for me. That was it! I could go.

"I walked back to my room in a kind of daze. I didn't know what it was, but I knew that something had happened in that room upstairs. Bill had somehow connected with me. From that point on, my whole attitude about treatment was different. I wanted what Bill had. That was more than twenty years ago, and I have never since touched alcohol."

****

But Bill could also use "tough love" when he sensed that that was what was required. Here's another man's description of an encounter with Bill. This man had been among the first to graduate from the treatment centre in Omaha; he had met Bill there and also had had subsequent contacts with him at A.A. gatherings. He liked Bill and was impressed by his insights into the secrets of sobriety. Then, after a time, he had found that what he had earlier received at Eppley was fading. He writes about what happened:

> "After I had been sober about five years, I became very depressed. My serenity and peace of mind had disappeared. I wasn't going any place. My growth had come to a halt. My job was tedious and boring. I was irritable, and my relationship with my fellow employees was at a low ebb; (of course, they responded in kind.) I was dissatisfied with my boss and his policies. My self-pity was overwhelming.
>
> "I continued to go to A.A. three or four times a week, but I found that the meetings had lost their meaning and power. I had turned sour on the program. My personal problems were so overwhelming that I wasn't getting anything helpful out of A.A. I stopped my usual prayer and meditation routine. My relationship with God was almost gone. I had taken control of my life again, and I was nearly back to where I had been in my drinking days. During my five years of sobriety, I had never bothered to get a sponsor. I felt I could handle my own life. But now the roof was about to fall in, and I needed help.
>
> "I called Bill Crooks, and he told me to meet him in his office that very day at

noon. There, I told him my sad tale of woe, reciting all of my problems, putting all the emphasis on how I was being mistreated and how miserable others were making my life. When I had finished, Bill sat silently for a long time. After a minute or so, I thought that perhaps he hadn't really heard me, and so I started to recite my list of woes for a second time.

"Bill stared at me; and then, with a resounding crash, he slammed his fist on his desk. He said in a loud and agitated voice, "God's will *will* be done!" I sat there stunned. I didn't know if he was angry at me or if he was just trying to get my attention. Bill tore into me. He lectured me on my self-will, my self-pity, my ego-driven concerns. He made it clear that my problems were all of my own making. He said that my main problem was that I had been drifting away from God. He also told me very clearly that I needed to have a sponsor.

"That encounter with Bill gave a jump-start to my work, my recovery program, and my relationship with God. I began again to grow spiritually -- and what a great feeling that was! I did get a wonderful sponsor. And I shall ever be grateful to Bill Crooks for what he did for me in 'telling it like it was'."

****

Bill could be strong and firm when that approach was required. He had no time for excuses. Whatever stood between a person and recovery had to be cut away; half-measures would not do.

> "I knew Bill Crooks both when I was drinking and after I stopped drinking -- and Bill Crooks knew me on both side of that fence. He also knew my wife. Before I got into A.A., Bill had told my wife, 'You've given your husband enough leeway, maybe too much! As much as I don't like divorce, you may to have to consider it for your own sobriety!'
>
> "Luckily, it didn't come to that.
>
> "In my recovery, I told Bill that I had taken the Fourth and Fifth Steps, (*ie.* writing out a fearless moral inventory, and confessing all that was in that inventory to God and another human being.) These are major steps for most people; Bill was surprised to hear that I had completed them for I had been in A.A. for only a month.
>
> "When Bill found out that I done these steps superficially, really in little more

than two short paragraphs, he said that he wanted to see me the following Monday. He promised that he would have something to help me do a complete Fourth Step. On that Monday, he handed me the Hazelden Analysis sheets.

"After three months of using that analysis and thus being forced to take an honest look at myself -- my inner self, the real self that I had previously revealed to no one, not even to myself) -- and after writing down all my discoveries, I showed the large stack of my 'confessions" to Bill and said to him, 'That's my Fourth! Sometime in the future, I'll be taking my Fifth.' He looked at me and said, 'That's great! Since you're willing, how about next Thursday at 2.00 p.m.? Yes, I'll see you in the Conference Room next Thursday at 2.00!' Thus, Bill forced me to take the Fifth. I know that, at the back of my mind, I had been intending to postpone that step indefinitely.

"Bill Crooks was certainly God's messenger in my sobriety!"

****

Many times, people did not fully recognize their personal needs until they met Bill.

They came to him, thinking, perhaps, that they had only a minor character flaw, no great problem, certainly nothing that required drastic spiritual surgery. Or, perhaps, they held the illusion that it was a loved one, a child, a marriage partner, who was the difficulty and that they, themselves, needed no "fixing". Many such persons found that an encounter with Bill Crooks brought changes they had not anticipated.

> **"I was so discouraged and depressed about our family situation. From all appearances, most people would have assumed that we were living 'the American dream'-- a big new house, two new cars, a boat, a cleaning lady, and a successful dental practice that was financing it all. But behind the walls, we knew the truth.**
>
> **'We had the best-stocked bar in the neighbourhood, and my husband was the one who enjoyed it most. He didn't drink in the mornings or during the day; but almost every evening, before he went to bed, he was drunk. With the alcohol came the personality change. Some nights he would be outgoing and funny; on other nights, he would be angry over almost nothing, screaming, swearing, calling us names, and having temper tantrums. We never knew on any night whether he would be Jekyll or Hyde. I**

had no hope that anything could ever be different.

"I entered Alanon for help; it was at my third Alanon meeting that I learned that a guest speaker had been invited to our group. I was told that he was an alcoholic from the Eppley Treatment Centre. I didn't want to stay to hear an alcoholic talk about drinking. After all, my husband wasn't an alcoholic: he just drank too much. I was attending Alanon simply to learn how I could make him cut down on his drinking. At that time, my concept of an alcoholic was of someone who had really hit bottom, someone who drank all the time and could not hold a job. I was really disappointed, therefore, to learn that one of "them" was going to speak to us that afternoon.

"When Bill Crooks entered the room, I was surprised to see that he was a strikingly handsome man with grey hair and deep blue eyes. He was smartly dressed in a grey suit and looked very much like a successful business man, not at all like the sort of person I had imagined would be coming from the Eppley Centre to address us. That was a real surprise!

"And then he started to talk. I had never before heard a man share his life story with such openness and humility; nor had I ever heard anyone express such deep belief in the power of God to perform miracles in the lives of people who completely give themselves to Him. Bill had the most penetrating blue eyes I had ever seen; they seemed to reflect a deep spirituality.

"After Bill had finished his talk and left the room, I found that I had some very different ideas about alcoholism and alcoholics. I was confused about how all these applied to my family's situation; but, if this man who had shared so openly about his life was an alcoholic who had recovered, I felt that just maybe there was an answer for my husband, too. If anyone who had lost so much, including the recent loss of a son, could still have such faith and inner peace, maybe there was hope for us. Maybe there was hope for me.

"A few weeks after the Alanon meeting, I entered the three-week outpatient Family Program at Eppley. It was a new program, and Bill was the therapist. There were only five in our group, and so the sessions were fairly intense. I thought that I was there to take notes and ask questions and learn about alcoholism and the program of recovery. I had no idea what I was in for.

"The first day, during our first group therapy session, one of the girls was talking lightheartedly, joking about one of her husband's drinking bouts. After a few minutes of listening to her bantering, Bill stopped her with his steely blue eyes. 'You're a phony,' he said. 'What's so funny about all that pain you feel when your husband gets into his heavy drinking?' The whole room was quiet. I could hear everyone gasping. I was shocked that he had confronted her like that. I held my breath. He just kept looking at her with those penetrating blue eyes; I had the feeling that he was looking into her very soul. She started to cry. She cried harder and harder, and Bill just sat there letting her hurt. I didn't understand what he was doing. I wanted to go to her and comfort her, but I sensed that that wouldn't be the right thing to do.

"After what seemed to be a long, long time, Bill started to talk to her in a low, comforting voice. His words were about her pain, about her life and her struggle to try to straighten out her life by herself and about the peace she would have if she let it all go and surrendered her life to God. He moved closer to her, took her hands in his, looked into her eyes, and gently asked her if she were ready to give up the battle, ready to ask God to take over her life, trusting Him to do a better job than she was doing. She tearfully nodded, yes, and he continued holding her hands and looking at her, a slight smile on his face. He had such a sense of peace and calm about him; we could all feel the presence of God in the room that day.

"That group therapy experience was a turning point in my life. I suddenly realized that I had never found a relationship with God like that. I had never trusted God with my whole life, but had always been running my life on my own, with a little help on the side from God. This idea of totally surrendering to God was so frightening, but I could see the peace and the Holy Spirit in Bill. His eyes were filled with it. I wanted that for my own life.

"A few days later, those deep eyes were turned on me, and I was on the 'hot seat' When Bill asked, 'How are you?' he didn't want to hear, 'Okay'. I knew by his eyes that he expected me to tell him how I really was. He didn't bother with small talk or idle chatter but cut to the very soul. I found my defences and my composure collapsing. I started to cry. I didn't realize that I had so much pain and anger. That night, I cried all night and seriously considered dropping out of the program. The next morning, with my eyes badly swollen, I looked worse than I can ever remember, but I decided to go back and face Bill again. Again, Bill was kind and gentle, not confrontational. I knew that I had really hit my own "bottom" and was ready to give up. That day I felt a peace I had not ever before known, a certainty that my life was in God's hands, and an absolute trust that God would take care of me in the future.

"Bill never pushed his Christianity on anyone. He simply shared his own experiences and gave just enough information that we had to search for ourselves. He told of how he rose early each morning to read his Bible. I wanted to reach his level of spirituality, and so I started to do the same thing. When one of the women asked what could explain what had happening in our group during our three weeks together, Bill told her to read the second chapter of the Book of Acts in the Bible. Bill never spoon-fed us the answers but always guided us on our own search for God.

"After our three-week program, Bill started a follow-up group of weekly meetings which he led. There were about twelve of us who attended. We shared our lives at a very deep level. Then, at Thanksgiving time, we heard the tragic news that Bill's daughter, Carol, had been killed. As a mother, I couldn't imagine the pain of losing two children, one right after the other. I expected that Bill and his wife would be utterly incapacitated, numbed by their grief.

"To my utter amazement, Bill was at our next meeting. He was sad, but he talked openly with us about Carol and her death. He told us how Marion and he had prayed together. He said that they were grateful for the good memories and happy times that they had had with Carol. He reminded us that our children don't belong to us: they are God's gifts to us; they belong to God and are entrusted to us only for a time. In all my life, I have never felt so moved as when he shared with us his joy and his grief in Carol's life and death. Only a person with a far closer relationship with God than mine could ever talk about God's goodness and love within the context of such a tragedy.

"Bill was a spiritual role model for me. We started a Christian Women's Bible Study and invited our Alanon and A.A. women friends to attend. For two years, we met in each other's homes, studying several books of the Bible. Some of us have maintained the very close spiritual friendships that developed from those studies, and we have grown even nearer to one another as the years have passed and our lives have changed. Bill's words and example are still with us, and we have often reminisced about 'the old days' and about how 'Bill would have said this'... or 'Bill would have suggested that ...'

"Bill Crooks life was truly a gift to us. His willingness to wade through all our subterfuge to reach the root of our problems, his courage in confronting us as individuals within a group, his readiness to disclose his own personal failings, his strong spirituality, his deep faith which he shared so openly, his bringing of hope to seemingly hopeless situations -- all these qualities were what made him so special a friend, confidant, counsellor, and spiritual leader.

"Bill's gift was his ability to see through a person's defences to the very soul. He didn't just talk about principles; he exposed our feelings. It's hard to describe how he did this, but we all saw it happening over and over again in our group. He would hold up a mirror and force the person to see himself or herself; he wouldn't allow us to escape with easy rationalisations or weak excuses for our behaviour.

"Unlike most counsellors, Bill wasn't content simply to listen to us and then to reflect back to us what he had heard us saying. Nor did he allow us take the lead, struggling among ourselves to solve our own problems through 'talking it out.' Bill knew that he was dealing with people whose lives were not grounded in spiritual principles; we were people who needed a clear path to follow, people whose lives were disasters. We didn't know how to find our way by ourselves. He tore down our defences. He made us vulnerable -- a very painful process. He showed us what we were doing that wasn't working. He gave us hope that, by following the Twelve Steps, we would find a new direction for living. And he kept reinforcing that everything hinged upon our taking the First Step: 'We admitted that we were powerless . . .' Admitting our powerlessness: that was the great essential.

"Bill wasn't afraid to reach out and touch people physically. He would hold your hands when you were in pain -- and his was always a healing touch, transmitting his own acceptance, strength, and faith to you. With Bill as leader, group therapy was never surface chatter, but a deep 'peeling of the onion' which removed all our defences. It was painful, and there were lots of heavy emotions -- anger, fears, resentments, deep hurts -- but he was comfortable with allowing people to experience those feelings. He was confident at such times because he knew that God could use him to bring healing. He was able to lead shattered lives to the God who would give them wholeness and an inner peace."

* * * * * * *

This theme is a recurring testimony from Bill's patients: he knew them better than they knew themselves. Bill had a gift for cutting away all the camouflage in which they had wrapped themselves, forcing them to look at who they really were. "Phoniness" couldn't exist in his presence. His patients learned that the experience of discovering and acknowledging one's true self could be both painful and liberating; always the experience was deeply spiritual; sometimes it brought about deeply religious experiences.

"My arrival at the Eppley Treatment Centre was by the 'back door'. Actually, I went through 'out-patient treatment' six times in eighteen months before I recognized that I, too, was an alcoholic. In those 'early' days in 1973 -- (I didn't get sober until 1975), Bill often sat in on the group therapy sessions. These were held in what we called 'the upper room'. The rooms on the lower level were more like hospital rooms with bright overhead lighting, but 'the upper room' had a much more intimate atmosphere with carpeting, couches, chairs, and lamps turned down low.

"When Bill was in our circle, he usually was silent and simply observed while a counsellor led the session. At first, having him there made me nervous since I knew that he was the clinic director; gradually, I became accustomed to his presence. I began to feel, however, that when Bill was with us, I would spend more than my share of time in the 'hot seat'. I don't know if that was truly the case or not; but I do know that on one memorable occasion, Bill, himself, put me on the 'hot seat'.

"In my treatment, counsellors had sometimes asked me how I felt about something, and I had always replied in terms of, 'My husband says . . .', or 'My father feels . . ." But how did I, myself, feel? I hadn't a clue. Not only didn't I know how I felt; I didn't even know what I thought. Counsellors would try to probe deeper: 'Not your husband or your father, but how do *you, yourself* feel? What do *you, yourself* think?" At such moments, I was honestly stumped. I wasn't aware of my feelings and thoughts. As a little girl, whenever I had expressed my emotions or put forward my ideas, I had been discounted or rebuked or punished. I had learned to suppress everything; and now it was like resurrecting the dead to discover who I really was.

"In the session that I recall so vividly, Bill was questioning me to explore what I was feeling and thinking. I remember being embarrassed by all the attention I was receiving -- and from Eppley's Director, no less! I was crying, sobbing, almost hysterical, a real mess! Then Bill said something. Strangely, I can't recall what it was, but Bill said something that triggered an image in my mind that melted away all my defences. In that instant, I fell back on the couch as a most profound sense of peace overtook me. What was that image? I saw a nearly forgotten picture which had hung in my grandmother's house, that famous picture of Jesus knocking at a door that has its latch only on the inside.

"I knew now what Bill had been getting at! I had to let God into my life. I, and I alone, had to do it God wouldn't or couldn't enter unless I opened the door. It was suddenly all so simple. I knew that what had happened in that instant was that I had at last opened the door and Jesus had come in, filling me with His gift of peace. I remained speechless, slumped on the couch. The group also remained silent for what seemed to me to be a very long time, probably more than five minutes. Then Bill got up and quietly left. Something very sacred had taken place. My real healing had begun that day.

"It's surprising, perhaps, that my recovery was rooted in such a strongly spiritual awakening because as a child I had had little or no religious training. Once, when I was eight, I had attended a Vacation Bible School near our farm; I had been taught some Bible verses and had been baptized. For a time after that, I had felt that I was 'saved' and that God was close to me. My parents weren't church-going, however; and I got the distinct feeling that they didn't very much like church-going people and gradually my 'sense of salvation' had vanished.) Then as a 'teen, I had occasionally accompanied a girl friend to a Catholic church, and after that I had often longed someday to be a Catholic myself; (just four years ago, I fulfilled that desire and converted to Catholicism.) Such experiences, though few and scattered, had helped me through a tough childhood; when, for example, my father would beat me unfairly and harshly, insisting that he would whip me until I cried, I would think, 'You can kill me if you want, but I will not cry! You aren't my real father! I have a Father in heaven.' My faith, though feeble and frail, had been there to sustain me through such experiences.

"There, in treatment, the faith came back to me again, giving me the spiritual insight that I so deeply needed; for, you see, by the time I had entered treatment, all my thoughts and feelings about God had faded almost entirely away. My faith was virtually gone. After I had married, I had never once thought of asking God to help me. I don't know why -- maybe my starting to drink had had more to do with the absence of God than had the fact I was unhappily married. But, in that one instant in that therapy session, Bill led me back into the presence of God and started the healing process that I so desperately needed."

****

This Higher Power to whom Bill introduced people was always loving, forgiving, life-changing. A "fire-and-brimstone" Judge, eager to throw sinners into hell, didn't enter Bill's thoughts. He knew that the people who came to him for help were already living in their own hells. His task was to bring them release.

"I remember the great load of guilt that I carried around inside me, guilt that crushed me, guilt that made me want to drink, guilt that came when I did drink. In treatment, I had to face my guilt. I felt so guilty that I thought I should be locked up in prison. I felt so guilty that I wanted to make atonement for all that I had ever done wrong. I don't remember exactly what Bill said. I just remember his being there and how, with him, I began to realize that I didn't need to be punished and I didn't have to make atonement. I began to realize that the past had passed, and that my life could begin again.

"I had always been so much in awe of Bill. He had such charisma! He seemed to me like a famous person, a Hollywood

star or something, someone who was godlike. I was terribly embarrassed to have this wonderful man see me as such a mess! But when I told Bill all that was on my conscience and revealed my tremendous guilt, I somehow felt as though he was the grandfather who had loved me so much when I was a child. I felt forgiven. I knew that Bill very much cared for me and very much loved me. That knowledge was exactly what I needed at that time."

* * * * * * *

Although he didn't admit it even to himself, Bill was a powerful public speaker. His lectures, both inside and outside his clinics, had a deep impact on many people. Not that he was a trained orator! Not at all. Always, he spoke quietly and humbly, never trying to draw attention to himself. Eloquence was not his goal. His only intent was that his listeners should accept the facts he was presenting to them and find the healing that God was offering them. People listened because he spoke the truth in love, and because he freely shared his personal story with them.

"Bill was important in my recovery. In 1973, I was in the Eppley Centre in Omaha. I had gone there for all the wrong reasons, but I eventually found that I couldn't lie to the staff without being called on my dishonesty; I learned, too, that I couldn't set my own rules (although I secretly continued to think of myself as being 'special' or 'unique'.)

The turning point in my attitude towards treatment came the first time that I heard Bill Crooks speak. He gave us a powerful lecture about the fact that alcoholism is a real disease. That message struck home, largely because of the man who gave it. There was this handsome guy up at the front. He was very credible and very convincing. He made it clear to us that he knew the truth of what he was saying because he, himself, had been there!

"He told us that day that our disease was progressive. I listened. I learned that, if I quit drinking, didn't touch a drop again for another twenty years, but then returned to drinking, my alcoholism wouldn't simply revert to what it had been when it first started; nor would it even revert to what it had been when I had quit. No, it would now be exactly as it would have been if I had continued drinking for those twenty years that I had been dry! In other words, even in those twenty years when I had not been drinking, the disease would have been progressing. That was a very, very frightening concept.

"Bill's lecture was so forceful that it marked a turnaround in my attitude towards treatment. I owe a great debt of gratitude to him. (Incidentally, I have just celebrated my 26th birthday in A.A..)"

* * * * * * *

But, as effective as Bill was as a speaker, his greatest power lay in the personal touch which he had on individual lives. He would know what to say -- and what not to say -- to bring a person to a realisation of the truth. Often, Bill would not have to say or do anything, but simply to "be": his presence seemed to radiate the love of God.

"Bill and I go back to 1974 when I was a suffering, bottomed-out alcoholic who (as a last resort, short of death) had resigned myself to going to Eppley in search of an 'overnight cure' for my disease.

"After five days in detox, I was moved into the unit and slowly began to gain some grasp on reality. I noticed a handsome silver-haired man on the unit and in the lectures. At first, I didn't have any idea who he was or what he was doing there. What struck me then, even in my fogged and confused state, was his sense of serenity: he seemed to exude an aura of calm and peace and inner joy and contentment, something I had always wanted and searched for all my life. His blue eyes, though piercing, were soft and gentle; I felt a sense of trust which I had never before experienced. When I looked at him, I immediately felt safer, more secure, less anxious. Without saying a word to me, he was passing on the precious gifts of spirituality and love. He reminded me of "God, Santa Claus, and Grandmother", all rolled into one. Bill wasn't even aware that, just by being there, he was touching another human spirit and was helping her on her way to recovery."

* * * * * * *

Many people who became familiar with Bill's work were amazed at his steady, quiet flow of energy. Although he never seemed to be rushing and although he always made time for anyone who needed him, he somehow managed to pack three days' work into one. Here's one of many such observations about Bill:

"The Eppley Alumni Association sponsored an annual weekend retreat for ex-patients; this retreat was held at the Columban Fathers Retreat House in Bellevue, south of Omaha. Forty to fifty people attended these popular events, with men and women present in fairly equally numbers.

"The retreats began on a Friday evening and ran through Mass late Sunday morning. They consisted of whole group sessions interspersed with meetings of smaller groups. Usually, a number of counsellors from Eppley would give the major addresses to the whole group; the small group sessions were self-directed and counsellor-free. For many of us, these retreats were the most valuable single activity offered by the Alumni Association throughout the year.

"At the last retreat I attended, Bill Crooks was the sole counsellor. Whereas usually four or five counsellors would have been on hand, Bill was there by himself. He gave five powerful lectures in that one weekend, and he also made himself available to many, many individuals who requested one-on-one sessions with him. The lectures he gave were totally spontaneous and free-wheeling, very much like conversations that were taking place between his head and his heart. I envied him his confidence and his ability to stand up before a group and speak with the freedom he did.

"I was especially impressed that Bill was willing to undertake such a heavy assignment singlehandedly. He seemed to do it easily, but it was obvious that he did not do it lightly. Beyond what he said, he modelled for all of us a cool and level-headed way of dealing with very complex and threatening subjects. He did well, and I am sure that he wanted to do well -- but he did not strive to be a dazzling communicator who would leave his listeners spellbound by his oratory. Instead of attempting to be the so-called 'perfect speaker', he wanted to reach each one of us with the message that God changes lives -- and, believe me, that he did!"

* * * * * * *

And so we see Bill pouring out his life for others, in public lectures and in private interviews, offering wounded souls the love of God, teaching and counselling, and always serving, helping, and healing. No wonder that people who came in touch with him came to believe that through Bill they had had contact with some "Higher Power"; through Bill, they had been enabled to sense the unconditional love of God. For them, Bill had made the Gospel credible: in the words of a familiar hymn, through Bill, they had discovered that their shattered lives had been "ransomed, healed, restored, forgiven."

CHAPTER SEVEN

"A MOST CHRISTLIKE MAN"

Whether they met Bill Crooks professionally or were introduced to him socially, many people left their encounters with him finding that they associated him with their image of what Jesus must have been like while He was on earth. Again and again, in telling of their impressions of Bill, they spoke in terms of Jesus. One man, for example, a mine supervisor, a "hard-nosed" engineer who prided himself on being a realist, once had a meeting with Bill about a business matter that had nothing whatever to do with alcohol or substance abuse. This man was a person known for being anything but "religious" in his approach to life. Yet from this quite ordinary meeting, the engineer emerged very thoughtful and subdued. The person who had arranged the interview for him asked what he thought. The engineer shook his head and said simply, "That man is the most Christlike person I have ever met!"

"Christlike" -- that is an adjective people repeatedly used to describe their encounters with

Bill. *Like Jesus, Bill brought a sense of God wherever he went.* Bill had none of the unfortunate trappings which many religious people carry about with them (and which drive so many of us away from organized religion.) Bill quoted no Scriptures; no pious phrases ever dropped from his lips. And yet, as was the case with Jesus, when people were in Bill's presence for any length of time, they came to a sense that something very "spiritual", something very "sacred" was in touch with them in this man's life. Bill brought them into an awareness of God. Many stories are like the following:

> "As I look back across almost thirty years, I realize how dysfunctional my life used to be. My days and nights were totally consumed with whatever was going on in my life at any moment. I had four small children and an alcoholic husband, and nothing was going right for me. Thus, I went to Al-Anon to sober up my husband and to get his life straightened out for him. What a rude awakening it was when I was told that I was there, not for my husband, but only for myself!
>
> "I was told that I needed to get 'fixed' and the best place in which to do that was probably in an outpatient program at Eppley. I knew that my

need was desperate. My sense of self-worth was nil. I was totally depressed. I couldn't make decisions for myself, seldom slept, hardly ate, and didn't want to go anywhere or see anyone.

"My life changed when I became involved with group therapy at the Eppley Centre, for it was there that I met a very special and godly man named Bill Crooks. Bill would sit in on our group. Sometimes, he would never say a word, but somehow you were certain that he knew what you were thinking and feeling -- and yet how could that be? Only God could do that! And yet Bill knew! He had the most penetrating but caring eyes that I have ever seen; he could see right through a person. At first, I felt afraid of him because I sensed that I couldn't get away with anything when I was with Bill. He was like no other person I had ever met. I had such a high respect for him that I was determined never to be a 'phony' when I was with him.

"One time, in therapy, after I had been explaining my feelings to the group, there was absolute silence from everyone in the circle. Then, Bill looked me straight in the face and said quietly, 'All you're doing is trying to get our sympathy.' At that, I suddenly broke down and cried and cried and cried. (Previously, I had told Bill that I was afraid to cry because I feared that I would never stop crying. Bill had said, 'Wouldn't that be okay?' Now I discovered what he had meant.)

"That day, I cried until I was all 'cried out'. And when that at last happened and my tears stopped, I simply surrendered my life to God and put Him at the very centre of my life. Bill asked me with a smile how I then felt, and I told him that the weight of the world had been taken off my shoulders. Bill then asked the rest of the group how they felt. They said that it seemed there had been a kind of 'whirlwind' in the room, a 'whirlwind' into which they all had found themselves drawn. It was a dramatic spiritual experience for them as well as for me. We had discovered what 'letting go and letting God' really meant. A bond of total trust was established between all of us in that group.

"Sometimes, at other group sessions, when someone felt that he or she could not 'open up' to those in the circle, Bill would start telling us about himself. He would tell us 'the good, the bad, and the uglies' of his own life; and invariably the person who had been emotionally blocked from sharing would find that he or she could also become as open and honest as Bill had been with us. Bill had shown us that it was safe for us to reveal our real selves.

"Bill could be so direct, and yet he could be so loving and caring at the same time. I've never known anyone like him; I've never been around anyone like him. There is no doubt in my mind that he was led by God to open the Eppley Centre. I am so grateful that I came to know Bill; if I had not known him, I don't know where I would be today. God reached me through Bill Crooks."

* * * * * * *

"Christlike" -- then, too, *like Jesus, Bill was a realist who saw people as they were and yet who always believed in what they could become.* Like Jesus, he regarded no one as hopeless, even those who themselves feared that they were beyond redemption. Here is one man's account of his encounter with Bill.

"When I went into the CDU in Jackson, I had given up, totally, completely. My family had long before washed their hands of me. I had been through treatment more than a dozen times without any positive results. I had fallen as low as a man can get and had been living on the streets, surviving by begging and sometimes stealing. I had been in and out of psychiatric hospitals and prison. I was sure I would never get better. For some reason, however, a judge gave me the choice of another jail sentence or another attempt at a clinic. I chose the clinic because the food was better.

"I discovered, however, that getting into the Jackson CDU was not easy. I was in my forties and hadn't worked since I was twenty. I was known to all the staff; most of them believed that I was beyond help. I smelled something terrible; I hadn't bathed in months; my clothes could have walked away of their own accord. I was so far gone that I couldn't hold a knife and fork: I had to lap my food off the plate just as would a dog.

"But Bill admitted me. Although he didn't often get involved in the intake procedure, he heard about this 'awful case' and came to see me in the admissions office. He asked that we be left alone. Then, when the others were gone, he looked into my eyes for a long, long time. His eyes seemed to be talking to me. I wanted to look away because I was ashamed and embarrassed, but he held me with his eyes.

"And then he began to talk to me about what he saw. He told me about how much I was hurting. He said that, in his own way, he had been where I was. He described the sort of feelings I was having and told me that I was not a bad man -- just a very sick man. He said that God specialized in working with people like me. He told me that I would get better and that he was going to admit me to his unit. For the first time in a long time, somebody believed in me; and for the first time in a long time, I found myself hoping that I could get better.

"That was the turning point in my life. In the weeks that followed, a miracle began to happen. My life -- not my old life but a new life, better than I could have imagined -- was given to me. I have not used alcohol or drugs since that day. I am clean, sober, and happy. I have remarried, returned to school, and am

now employed. My disease is arrested. I have recovered. I owe everything to God and to Bill Crooks."

* * * * * * *

"Christlike": *like Jesus, too, Bill always put an individual's need above every other concern.* So often, in the Gospels, one reads of Jesus, stopping whatever He was doing to respond to a cry for help. So often, He changed his schedule or interrupted His plans in order to meet someone's immediate need. Bill was like that. He was prepared to drop whatever he was doing in order to deal with any situation which unexpectedly arose. There are many stories about Bill like the following:

"It was 1975, and I had been sober a full year. Thanks to God, Bill Crooks, and the staff at Eppley, I was experiencing a glorious and rewarding sobriety. I had been reborn! I was experiencing Life with a capital 'L'. My husband and I had renewed our marriage vows. Our daughters were 15, 13, and 9. I was active in the A.A. fellowship and was eager to learn all I could. Times were good.

"At this time, Bill was conducting a week-long workshop in Crete, Nebraska, a town about 90 miles from Omaha. I had

decided to attend because Bill was my mentor, and I was like a sponge. On Sunday, my husband had driven me to Crete and had helped me settle in. (Being away from home and family for a full week was a 'big deal' for me!)

"The workshop went well. On Thursday evening, however, I was haunted by a strange compulsion to call home. I called and, to my grief and horror, learned that my 13-year-old had been raped while she was baby-sitting. (She had put herself in harm's way in order to protect the two small children under her care.) At the time I called, my husband was with her in emergency.

"The instant Bill heard about what had happened (without my asking him and without a second thought on his part), we were in his car, heading back to Omaha. By the time we reached the house, my husband and daughter were back from the hospital. She was all right physically, but she was deeply traumatised: her emotional wounds would take a long time to heal.

"That night, before returning to Crete to complete the week's seminar, Bill took a long time arranging for my daughter to have counselling and group therapy to

help her deal with her horrible experience. And (as only Bill could and would), he spent an equally long time with my husband and me, making sure that we were all right, before he drove the 90 miles back to his work. It was long after midnight before he left our house."

* * * * * * *

"Christlike": *also, like Jesus, Bill had the gift of spiritual insight.* A reader may have noticed how often in these stories about Bill people have spoken of his searching eyes which seemed able to read their souls. Like Jesus, Bill could pierce the outer shell and see what was really happening in the heart. The experience of having Bill "read one's soul" could at times be uncomfortable and unsettling.

"In the months following treatment, as my wife and I were trying to find our way through one of the many readjustments that recovering couples have to make, I mentioned to Bill that I was having a problem in the marriage. He told me to make an appointment for my wife and me to meet him in his office. We did this and, one afternoon soon afterwards, arrived at the clinic. When we entered the room, he was on the 'phone; but he waved us to take a seat. I

remember that he seemed to be swamped with work; the 'phones kept ringing; his secretaries kept bringing him messages. Finally, he called a halt to the 'busyness', switched off his 'phones, closed the door, and turned to us.

"There was, perhaps, one moment of chit-chat. He then said to my wife that I had told him why we were there: (it was a very delicate and personal issue.) Then, he turned to me and asked quite simply, 'Do you believe that this Twelve Step program works?' 'Yes,' I replied. He said nothing more but held my eyes with his. I couldn't look away. He said nothing with his lips, but his eyes were saying to me, 'You and I know exactly what I am saying to you, don't we? You know what the real problem is, and you know the answer.' Then, after this longest moment of my life, his face relaxed and mine did, too. There was a silence, and then I realized that the interview was over. With that, we left.

"I would like to add that story to the list of many other stories of near-miracles performed by Bill Crooks. I guess the story doesn't qualify; but then, again, maybe it does. I went to Bill's office, hoping for an easy miracle; instead, Bill

gave me a strong dose of reality -- which, I suppose, was the only kind of miracle that could have helped."

* * * * * * *

"Christlike": *like Jesus, Bill's love was not simply for people in general, but for people in particular, person by person by person.* However well things might be going within his clinics in general, he was most concerned for his patients as individuals. Stories abound about Bill's work with patients -- stories about how he always walked "the second mile" with them, stories about how sometimes he was far more concerned with helping them than they were concerned for their own recovery.

"One night, I attended a board meeting for the Eppley Alumni Association. Bill was supposed to be present; but, just as the meeting opened, he 'phoned to say that he was working with a patient on the unit upstairs and he would be late. We were to go on without him. Two hours went by, and Bill at last appeared. He was obviously exhausted. He told us that the patient had gone into denial and had wanted to check out of treatment. He said that he had used every tool he had (and Bill had every tool there was), but the man had finally stormed out. What struck me was how genuinely

distressed Bill was. Although he had done his best, he was hurt and saddened and was very, very tired. I was reminded of a Bible story, that one about a shepherd who, although he had ninety-nine other sheep in his flock, was so concerned because one had gone missing."

****

Christlike -- *like Jesus, Bill set no limits on whom he would help or on what form his help would take.* Far beyond his professional work in his clinics, Bill still reached out to others who were in any kind of need. Just as when he worked in the family business, so when he worked in his clinics Bill never felt he was "off-duty". Anyone who needed help he would help even if such assistance had nothing whatever to do with his professional responsibilities.. The fact that he and Marion had gone through great tragedy had only made both of them more willing and better able to minister to others. Because of their bereavements, for example, they received so many special calls for service.

"I had left the treatment centre in April, sober and happy, grateful to have been given a new way of life. All was going perfectly. Then, in August, my world fell apart. Our son was killed in an aeroplane

crash. To whom could we turn for help? Immediately, we thought of Bill and Marion; we knew that they could relate to our grief because they had lost both Paul and Carol. We telephoned, and they both came to us immediately. They stayed at our side through the long days and nights that followed. We knew that we were not alone.

"Those first contacts developed into a lasting friendship that became almost like family. Like my husband, Bill was a sailing enthusiast; we had a sail boat and many Saturdays saw the four of us together at the lake. Bill helped my husband build a fine boathouse; carpentry was another of his many gifts. We had many opportunities to observe Bill when he was far, far away from his duties at the hospital. We knew why he was so successful: on or off the job, he fully lived the Twelve Steps. A.A. was his way of life."

* * * * * * *

Christlike: *like Jesus, too, Bill always had a spiritual intuition about where he should go and what he should do.* Earlier in this book, we came upon instances of Bill's supernatural guidance -- his sudden catching of a 'plane to prevent a friend's suicide, or his following an impulse to write a letter to a student minister who at that time very much needed to receive that message. These direct insights into what had to be done continued with Bill throughout his life: there are numerous accounts of how he was moved to 'phone or write or visit a person precisely at the moment that such a contact was most needed. The following is a typical story:

> "I had had two years of sobriety and was doing pretty well. Then I lost my brother. I hadn't realized how much I had really loved him until he was gone. I knew that I needed a drink. I simply had to start drinking again, I told myself. I decided that I was going to drink steadily for the next three months. (Why I came up with the notion of a three-month spree, I have no idea.) I was in such grief that I had to promise myself that alcohol was waiting there to take away my pain. Out of respect for my brother's memory, however, I decided to postpone my drinking bout until after his funeral.
>
> "Then, out of the blue, Bill 'phoned. His timing was perfect! He had heard about my loss and was calling to see how I was doing. I didn't mention my plans to return to drinking, but I told him that I wasn't doing all that well. I thought that Bill would express his sympathy at my sorrows. Instead, he said unexpectedly,

'Look, you've got to surrender everything!' I remember wondering, 'What does he mean? What has surrender to do with this?'

"After the 'phone call, I went upstairs and closed myself in the bedroom. Then it hit me! Bill had sensed how I was thinking. He was telling me that God could not help me with my pain while I was planning to use alcohol as a way to escape my pain. If God was going to be able to heal me, I had to get rid of all idea of an easy and artificial 'way out'. I turned to God at that moment, and I put my broken heart in His hands. A deep peace immediately came over me. I was released from my grief. And I knew that, for the rest of my life, if I would only keep my life surrendered to Him, God would meet my every need."

* * * * * * *

"Christlike" -- *a description not only of Bill but of the remarkable woman whose own surrendered faith made his special ministry possible.* So many tell of the influence she had on them through Bill.

"When I found myself in treatment, I was madder than hell because I didn't want to be there. My husband had dragged me there. And it was while I was in that mood that I first met Bill Crooks. I was very agitated and I walked up to him and demanded, 'What am I going to do here?' He said, 'You're going to take a really good look at yourself,' and then walked away. I thought, 'Darn, this is going to be different than the other places I've been.' I had been involved with psychiatric therapy for year after year after year. (I think my psychiatrist drank almost as much as I did.) I had been in many psychiatric wards and clinics, but they had never done me any good.

"This time was different. Bill personally saw to it that I went through the program step by step. He saw to it that I didn't take any half-measures. My recovery had to be thorough and complete. And when my weeks on the unit were at last over, he wouldn't let me go home. He assigned me to Santa Monica, a halfway house that had just been purchased. It was at Santa Monica that I first met Marion. Despite her great handicap, she was there, helping to paint the walls and the ceiling. For all of us who were recovering addicts and alcoholics, she always had a gentle smile and a heart filled with love She became a close, dear friend.

"Bill and Marion were a great team together. You can't think of one without the other. They were like the two sides of a single coin; when you got Bill on one side, you found Marion on the other. I don't know if Marion ever received full credit for her part in all of Bill's successes. With her incurable illness, she would have had every right and reason to ask that Bill should curtail his work in order to spend more time with her; instead, she was as selfless as was Bill and allowed Bill to go on with his mission. People who received help from Bill usually didn't realize that Marion was also serving them through Bill. Bill and Marion were one and the same: Without her understanding and support, he could never have done all that he did. Like Bill's, her life was a living sermon on the love of Jesus."

* * * * * * *

"Christlike" -- like Jesus, Bill put God's will before all other considerations in his life. In 1981, after five years in Jackson, Bill was approached by the Eppley Centre in Omaha. In the years since he had been there, problems had developed. Some felt that the original focus of the program had been changed. Moreover, the Eppley Centre was now planning an expansion of its outreach programs and needed new direction. Thus, there was an

urgent request that Bill return at least for a time and help reactivate and strengthen the work. It was a very difficult decision for the Crooks to make. Their "support systems" were all in Jackson, and at this stage of Marion's illness that support was increasingly important. Much of the time, Marion was semi-bedridden and was requiring much care. The warm weather of Mississippi was good for both her body and her spirits; there she had access to a heated pool which made it possible for her to exercise. She and Bill knew that the cold of the Nebraska winters would complicate their lives and increase her discomfort. Nevertheless, they both sensed that a call of God lay in the request that had been made Reluctantly, Bill resigned his position in the Mississippi Baptist Hospital and with Marion returned to the Nebraska Methodist Hospital in June, 1981.

Back in Omaha and among his old friends, Bill was as busy as ever in his work at Eppley. In some ways, it felt like old times. Now, however, there were his ever-increasing responsibilities at home. Marion continued to be her brave and loving self. Whatever she was experiencing, she chose never to reveal her despondency in public. Always, she remained beautifully groomed, smiling, gracious, more concerned for others than for herself. Occasionally, she was able to participate in activities at the centre. There is one touching description of a rare appearance at a pot-luck supper held in connection with Eppley:

"Bill brought his wife to the supper. Marion Crooks had been ill for a long time with degenerative disease of nerves and muscles. She was rarely seen by anyone. This was the only occasion on which my wife and I ever met her.

"Bill lifted Marion up from the seat of their car and carried her into the house and set her down in a chair. I remember that she could scarcely move and that one arm was propped straight out in an extended position by a sophisticated contraption of rods and cords. As the evening went on, Bill had to help his wife continually to change her positions in order that she could remain comfortable.

"Bill and Marion never alluded to her difficulties. They handled themselves easily, obviously reflecting the fact that what we were witnessing was their regular way of coping with her condition. They were so natural about the situation that the rest of us were soon put at ease. We pretty much behaved as we would have done had there been no problem at all. Yet it was a most moving experience."

That was probably the last time that Marion was to be outside the home in Omaha. And Bill continued his work at Eppley and his equally demanding work at home. He had little time to himself; and, when he did, he turned to his faith for his power and his peace.

"It happened that Bill Crooks attended the same church I did. He would always come in and sit alone. He seemed to want it that way. We would have a cordial greeting, but no more. He always left the building immediately after the service. I feel sure that he was hurrying home to be with Marion. I noticed that, apart from greeting people he knew, Bill Crooks was always silent in church. It struck me that he came to church just to listen and receive. He was there for his own spiritual renewal."

* * * * * * *

"Christlike" -- There is a moving verse in the Fourth Gospel, a verse which describes the faithfulness of Jesus' love for those who were closest to Him: "Jesus, having loved His own who were in this world, loved them unto the end." *Like Jesus, Bill, too, loved unto the end those who were his special own.* No marriage partner was ever given greater love or more tender care than

Marion received from Bill.

By September, 1985, Bill knew that he had done all he could to assist in Omaha. Marion's health was of increasing concern. The cold weather brought her discomfort; she missed the warm pool she had had in Mississippi, and she missed her close friends there. Bill returned Marion to Jackson, and there took a new position as Director of Program Development at the Baptist Hospital, initiating new programs in Jackson and across the state. Friends who welcomed them "home" were shocked to see how greatly Marion had failed during the time they had been gone: she was now little more than "skin and bones".

Through the CDU at the Mississippi Baptist Hospital, the *Alpha Association* had been formed as a support group for families of patients who were in recovery. Most members of this association knew Bill and Marion; many of them now volunteered to bring meals to the home and to stay with Marion for parts of every day while Bill was at work. Even with such help, however, all the major responsibilities fell on Bill. Barely able to move a muscle, Marion was confined to a "suspension bed", and was totally dependent on him for her every care. Bill spent every spare moment with her, cleaned the house, did the laundry, bought the groceries. Often in the evenings, she was in great pain, and on those occasions he stayed up with her, sometimes all night, until she fell asleep.

    Bill's brother and sister-in-law, Jamie and Mabel, made two trips from Thunder Bay to Jackson to determine ways in which they could help[9]. They were distressed by Marion's condition -- but almost equally distressed by Bill's appearance. He was pale, haggard, thin. They wondered to themselves how he could continue. Continue he did, however. Only once in that final dark year did Bill give way to despair. It was late at night. Marion had been violently ill. The bedding would have to be changed again. Bill had had no sleep the night before and was completely exhausted. He went into an adjoining room and fell to pieces. Breaking into uncontrollable sobbing, he cried aloud, "My God, my God, why have You forsaken me?" Then, regaining his composure, he returned to assist Marion and to clean the room. Typical of Bill, he felt badly about this moment of despair which he regarded as weakness. Later, he felt the need to confess the incident to his friends.

    Bill nursed Marion to the end, rarely leaving her side in the last weeks. She did not want to go to a hospital, and Bill respected her wishes. She died at home on June 10th, 1987, at the age of sixty-five.

---

[9]. Years earlier, Jamie and Mabel had come to realize that Bill had followed a true calling of God when he had left the family business to become a counsellor; they had become strong supporters of all that he was doing.

Memorial services were held in Jackson and in Thunder Bay. At Bill's special direction, the eulogies and messages in both those services emphasised how true and loving a helpmate she had been to Bill: without her faithful support and her own personal commitment to Christ, Bill could not have been so greatly used to help others. Marion's remains were laid to rest in Thunder Bay, in Riverside Cemetery, next to the bodies of Paul and Carol.

And now, for the first time all alone, this most Christlike man returned to Mississippi to resume his work.

CHAPTER EIGHT

"HE MADE US KNOW..."

The story of Bill's final years can be simply told. With Marion gone, he was freed from the home responsibilities that had weighed him down. Able now to do whatever he wanted, he found that what he wanted now even more than ever was simply to help others. He kept longer hours at the Baptist Hospital in Jackson, sometimes spending twelve hour days in his office developing new initiatives for dealing with chemical dependency. He undertook more personal counselling, making himself available to whoever was referred to him by doctors or by clergy. He accepted more speaking engagements, and several times each month found himself addressing service clubs, youth rallies, and conferences, not only in Jackson but across the state. Many wondered if he was keeping himself so busy because now he was so alone. And then, in October, 1987, only four months after Marion's death, Bill's responsibilities increased still further as he was appointed the Executive Director of the Jackson Recovery Centre, a forty-bed licensed hospital for chemical dependency patients.

Not, of course, that Bill was without friends at this time. So many people whom he and Marion had helped now wanted to help him in return. Among these was a slim, gentle, and attractive lady, Lanier Brooks. She had first met Bill in 1979 when her former husband had entered Bill's clinic. In the years that had followed, although her marriage had not survived, she had gone through a family treatment program under Bill's guidance and had come greatly to respect him as a counsellor and a speaker. She had worked as a volunteer in Bill's hospital and had come to know Marion well; before the Crooks had moved back to Omaha, she and Marion had belonged to the same bridge group. Then, after the Crooks had returned and Marion's health had swiftly declined, Lanier had been among those from the *Alpha Association* who had taken meals to the Crooks and had spent afternoons with Marion while Bill was at the office A strong friendship had developed between the two women. Lanier had come to admire and love Marion, and she had grieved with Bill as well as for him when Marion had died.

Bill and Lanier had much in common. Like Bill, Lanier was a committed Christian, thoroughly familiar with the Twelve Step Program, intent on developing her spiritual growth and life. Like Bill, she enjoyed the out-of-doors, walking, cycling, skiing, and (like Bill) especially tennis. In the months that followed, the two of them began to see more and more of each other; a deep friendship took root and blossomed. Slowly the conviction grew that God intended them to build a new life together. On October 1, 1988, Bill and Lanier were married in a quiet service atop a mountain near Asheville, North Carolina. Bill's friends who knew the special difficulties that had been his and how bravely he had borne them rejoiced at the news that he was to be no longer alone.

At the same time, Bill was convinced that the Jackson chapter in his book was finished, and that it was time to turn the page. Harold Hughes, a former senator and former governor of Iowa, knew personally of Bill's work and of the proven effectiveness of his treatment programs. Senator Hughes had long dreamed of establishing a series of private clinics for alcoholics throughout the Midwest, and many times he had discussed such a project with Bill. Now, learning that Bill was ready to leave Jackson, he offered him the position of becoming the director of the whole scheme, first setting up a primary clinic in Des Moines and then establishing satellite clinics across Iowa. It was an exciting challenge and one which Bill enthusiastically accepted. Following their wedding, he and Lanier took one month to holiday and to settle their affairs in Mississippi. They then moved to Des Moines to start a new home and a new career.

* * * * * * *

In November, 1988, Bill began to organise the clinic in Des Moines. Almost from the start, it became obvious that something was going wrong. The terms of reference began to change; for personal reasons, Mr. Hughes' interest in the project appeared to wane. The idea of satellite clinics at first was downplayed and then was dropped. Bill, who seldom was dismayed by anything, now found himself deeply discouraged. As the grand scheme into which he had been recruited continued to unravel, he became convinced that he could not continue. After six months he resigned: that resignation was far from an easy decision for either him or his new bride: it was far removed from the way in which they had thought that they would start their life together. Not knowing what they were to do, Bill and Lanier simply prayed and trusted God and waited for Him to guide them.

In April, 1989, during this time of waiting, Lanier returned to Mississippi to attend a son's wedding. Instead of accompanying her, Bill paid a visit to Thunder Bay to see Peter and the granddaughters and to spend time with his brothers and friends. Then, the unexpected occurred. A counsellor at the Smith Clinic tells about it.

"I was walking along Red River Road when whom should I meet walking towards me but Bill Crooks whom I had not seen for ten years! We stopped to chat. I learned that he had arrived in Thunder Bay only the day before. 'Oh,' I said, 'you're here about the job.' He looked puzzled. 'What job?' 'The directorship at the Smith Clinic. Our director has just resigned.' Bill got a funny look in his eyes and replied, 'I didn't know.'"

Bill thought that he could recognize the guidance of God when he heard it and made immediate enquiries about the position. Lanier wasn't quite so sure: the idea of 40 below winters in a land far from Alabama held no appeal. She asked him to look elsewhere; (in fact, she had already arranged interviews for him in Nashville, Tennessee.) But Bill's interviews at the Smith Clinic made it clear to him that that was where he was needed, and the Smith Clinic recognized that Bill's special gifts and long experience made him the person for whom they were searching. Lanier assented. (Later, she was to write that, after having seen what was happening in Thunder Bay, she recognized that their being in Canada was truly part of God's plan for them.) And so Bill found himself at the director's desk and in that very position which he and Sister Sharon had discussed almost twenty years earlier.

The work at the Smith Clinic went steadily forward under Bill's direction. The same miracles of life-changing took place. The same spiritual witness was made. Not only those troubled with problems of addiction but those looking for an answer to life came to Bill to learn his secret. Bill was glad to be back at the Smith, glad to be back with his family, glad to be able to become better acquainted with his two grand-daughters. Old friendships were resurrected, and Lanier became introduced to Bill's past. She even came to accept, almost without complaint, the long and bitterly cold winters as part of the cost of her "calling". The two of them were active in St. Andrew's Presbyterian Church, the church where, in the "Good Companions", Bill and Marion had met so many years before; they also were instrumental in forming a spiritual fellowship group in the home of friends.

In these years at the Smith Clinic, the only clouds in the Crooks' sky were concerns about Bill's health. For more than a year, a mole had been forming on Bill's abdomen, but he had been too busy to worry about it. In June, 1989, during a routine physical check-up, it was spotted and diagnosed as melanoma in its fifth (and most critical) degree. There was an immediate operation; the growth was deep, but the surgeons were pleased. They told Bill that he would need no further treatment because they had "got it all."

A second emergency arose with Bill's heart. Bill always had the body of an athlete and had always kept himself in top condition; during and after the war, he had smoked; but that addiction like his alcoholism had vanished after his conversion in 1963[10]. Now, however, he developed severe angina; an angiogram indicated that he was urgently in need of a coronary bypass; and he was put on a long waiting list for that surgery. The waiting stretched from weeks into months, and Bill's angina became increasingly unbearable. It was apparent that, unless something were done immediately, Bill would die. In 1990, he went to the Mayo Clinic in Rochester, Minnesota, and had a double by-pass. He made a quick and complete recovery, and so the health emergencies seemed to have vanished.

* * * * * * *

In 1992, aged 66, Bill retired from the Smith Clinic. He and Lanier hoped now to have more time for their friends and their family. They also wished to experiment with new ways to serve their Lord. They were able to lease a large, rugged,

---

[10] For the consolation of any reader who may be battling with smoking, it should be noted that even Bill had a long struggle with 'the weed'. (He always maintained that nicotine is a more powerful addiction than heroin.) Bill, however, refused to be beaten by tobacco, and eventually he found release. By the time he returned to the Smith Clinic, he had been tobacco-free for many years.

comfortably-furnished home in a dramatic country setting on a hilltop overlooking Lake Superior. They had a dream that this might be turned into a Christian retreat centre; the place seemed perfect for such an endeavour; and, in fact, several weekend workshops and conferences did come to be scheduled there. At first, Bill and Lanier had high hopes for their home with its cheerful name, "On Top of the Hill". In the two winters that followed, however, they came to realize that, on Bill's retirement income, it was impossible for them to maintain so large a house. And the warmth and sunshine of the South were calling to them both.

In May, 1993, after looking at several locations along the sunny beaches of the Gulf of Mexico, the Crooks moved their belongings to Gulf Shores, Alabama, where they planned to spend their retirement years together. They bought a house and found their niche in the community. Bill organized a large fellowship of seniors who made bicycling one of their activities and who became known around Gulf Shores as the "Old Spokes". The Crooks became extremely active in First Presbyterian Church in the nearby town of Foley: Bill was soon elected to the session. In that congregation, Bill spear-headed an every-home visitation to challenge members to take seriously the full implications of their faith; again, lives were changed and spiritual commitments were renewed. With the approval of the church's session, Bill launched a Twelve Step Program for Christians that had a deep impact on a number of lives; that group continues to meet today. Bill worked with the minister in promoting and leading "Cursillo", a lay-led retreat movement across Alabama. And with Lanier, Bill found enormous satisfaction in after-school, one-on-one tutoring of little children who needed special help.

In these retirement years, Bill finally found time for some of the simpler pleasures of life which he had always enjoyed but which he had so often postponed in his endless pursuit to serve others. From boyhood, Bill had always been sensitive to the beauty of nature, but now he had time with Lanier to walk the long sandy beaches at Gulf Shores, listening to the rhythm of waves, watching the splendour of the sun as it sank beyond the horizon. Now, too, he enjoyed "kibitzing" with friends and sharing memories of times past. (Here, as always, he chose more to listen than to speak. He never referred to his achievements; rather, he repeatedly expressed his real admiration for what others had accomplished in their careers. Bill had the habit of always turning a conversation away from himself to focus on others.) Bill also discovered that he was fond of working in the kitchen with Lanier, experimenting with new recipes, sampling new tastes. With Lanier, too, he welcomed a constant stream of friends: snowbirds explaining that they were fleeing the cold of Canada and Nebraska, or Mississippians claiming that they wanted to sample life on the Gulf. In truth, most of the people who visited to Gulf Shores came not for the weather but for the company. The Crooks had a knack for helping people to relax, making them feel at home. Much of the attraction was Bill's own "down-to-earth" simplicity: apart from his boundless love for others, Bill was in most other ways just an "ordinary guy", someone with no axe to grind, nothing to prove, and no need to impress those around him. This retirement calm seemed to be a fitting reward after a lifetime of devoted service. Bill and Lanier looked forward to many happy years together.

Lanier reports that in their quiet times together, Bill never mentioned the sacrifices he had made or the sorrows that life had brought him. Just as he was without any sense of personal pride in his career, so he was free of any trace of self-pity. Amazingly, his only thoughts about the years past focussed on a regret that he had not been able to do more to help others; he felt that he had not done enough. Bill never fully recognized the blessing he had been to so many. He never saw himself as "a man who had made a difference." Jesus once asked, "Why do you call Me good? There is none good but God!" Bill had the same humility as he looked back across his life.

* * * * * * *

In June, 1996, an x-ray revealed a small nodule in one of Bill's lungs: it was removed and a series of radiation treatments was administered. The doctors expressed deep concern but gave assurance that there was hope and that all might still be well. Bill, himself, was calm and confident. That summer, he and Lanier travelled to Thunder Bay to be with his family and friends. A highlight for Bill was a rugged canoe trip with Peter, a venture which involved long portages, endless treks through swamp and bush, clouds of black flies and mosquitoes. When at last they had reached the remote lake on which they were to camp and had set up their tent, Bill, bruised, bitten, and weary, stretched out on the rocks in the late afternoon sun and said contentedly, "Life just doesn't get any better than this!" Ever a "man's man", Bill meant it!

By the following February, it was obvious that life, in truth, wasn't getting any better but in fact was becoming much, much worse. Nodules had again appeared in Bill's lungs; these were removed, and there were more radiation treatments. The growths kept recurring, however; and by June they were erupting almost as quickly as they could be removed. Bill was discouraged but not yet defeated. Although the doctors believed that death was now inevitable, Bill thought that there might still be a chance if he subjected himself to the maximum possible dosage of chemotherapy

-- a brutal undertaking, but one on which he, himself, insisted. Because of the horrible side effects of the chemo, Bill could not remain in his house at Gulf Shores but had to enter the oncology wing of the Sacred Heart Hospital in Pensacola. Lanier stayed at his side. The chemotherapy was devastating, but Bill ordered it to be continued.

Despite the misery of these final weeks, there were good experiences for Bill. His younger brother and sister-in-law, George and Doris, were able to come for a few days of special visiting with him. Then Peter came for a whole week; the hospital made arrangements so that Peter could share his father's room. And from nearby Gulf Shores, there were so many friends who wanted to be with Bill, both to assure him of their love and still to enjoy his good company. Thus it was that, on July 29th, six of these close friends came to his hospital room to watch an afternoon of television tennis with him. Shortly after their visit, Bill seemed suddenly to "let go"; he gently slipped into unconsciousness to awaken in the arms of God.

* * * * * * *

Three memorial services were held -- in Foley, in Thunder Bay, and in Omaha. Large congregations attended each. Messages arrived from across the United States and from every province in Canada . . .

"Had it not been for Bill's leadership at Eppley, I would not be sane or even alive today."

"When I don't know what God wants me to do, I ask,'What would Jesus do?' But sometimes I am not sure what Jesus would do, and then I ask, 'What would Bill do?' Bill Crooks made God and Jesus real to me."

"When my husband died, I didn't know where to turn for help. No one seemed to know what to say to ease my pain. Bill knew. And Bill pulled me through."

"I always said that Bill could settle the dust in any room. All he had to do was walk through the door, and there was that feeling that 'Bill's here, and everything will be okay now.'"

"It was a privilege to work on the same staff with Bill. No one could have been a better friend or example..."

"Twenty-three years ago this month, Bill decided that I needed treatment. As a result of that decision I am alive and well today."

"Bill was very patient, very kind, very loving. He always took delight in what

was right, never in things wrong. He believed, hoped, loved, and endured in all circumstances and in all situations. His life had three abiding qualities: faith, hope, and love -- and the greatest of these was love."

Hundreds of such tributes arrived in the days following Bill's death, evidence that Bill's spirit was alive and well in those thousands of lives in which he had made a difference. On August 12th, 1997, on a quiet sun-filled afternoon, Bill's remains were laid to rest beside Marion's with Paul's and Carol's in the family grave in Riverside Cemetery, Thunder Bay. Peter placed his father's ashes in the grave. The minister whom thirty years earlier Bill had saved from suicide read the familiar words of Jesus, "Well done, good and faithful servant! Enter thou into the joy of thy Lord! Whoever loses his life for My sake and the Gospel's shall find it! Whoever would be greatest among you, let him be the servant of all. Inasmuch as you have done mercy and kindness to one of the least of My brethren, You have done it unto Me. And this is My commandment, that you love one another as I have loved you. Greater love hath no man than this, that he lay down his life for his friends." As those present remembered Bill, such statements took on special meaning.

* * * * * * *

Peter can give us our final glimpse of Bill.

"During his last year, Dad and I talked a lot with each other on the 'phone. And before that last year, we had enjoyed some of the best times of our lives together. Canoeing, skiing, fishing, and just 'hanging out' together, we had come to know each other all over again, not only as father and son but as best buddies. Those last times with him will remain in my 'memory bank' forever.

"He called me just before his chemotherapy sessions began. He said that he knew that he was under the care of God and that he was placing his life totally into the hands of his doctors. He was not afraid. I think, however, that it was actually the huge chemotherapy bombardment which killed him.

"I stayed with Dad for a full week at Sacred Heart Hospital in Pensacola; in that time, I was fortunate that, although he was not always aware where he was, he returned to reality for brief periods. The first night, I stayed in his room; he was fully alert. We talked for hours about nothing specific, just reminiscing about all the fun times we had recently had. At other times, when Dad was 'out of it', he talked a lot about the war, (something which he had never done before); he spoke about Albert Kelly and other old friends from the Royal Canadian Air Force. He didn't speak a lot about Mom, but at one point he seemed to feel that she was in the room with him.

"The time came when I had to leave the hospital to return to Thunder Bay. As I walked out of Dad's room, I realized that I would never see him again. I broke down in the hallway near his door. Then I remembered how strong he had always been through all his own tragedies, and I knew that I, too, could have that strength. I realized that I was not crying for him but for myself. He was in good hands. Dad knew that he was surely going on to a better place to be with Mom and Carol and Paul in Heaven. My tears stopped. I left the hospital with my own faith strengthened, and feeling unbelievably proud that Bill Crooks was my father.

"Now that he is gone, I think of him at the oddest times -- at night, for example, when my work takes me out to groom ski trails, or when I am camping up north, sleeping out under the stars. I look up at the vast universe and realize how insignificant my life would seem to me had I not known my father. As he did for everybody who knew him, he made me realize that I am loved by God. Dad did that for all of us who knew him -- he made us know that we are loved."

A FINAL WORD

"The world has yet to see what would happen if a man were to give himself completely to the service of Jesus Christ!" "Not so," we reply, "we knew such a man. His name was Bill Crooks."

Dietrich Bonhoeffer, the martyr hanged by the Nazis in April, 1945, was once asked to define who Jesus is for our modern world. Other ages have interpreted the importance of Christ as "the Second Person of the Trinity" or "the Word of God" or "the Crucified Lamb" or "the Prophet, Priest, and King" -- but what is His significance for us today? Bonhoeffer replied, "Today, Jesus is the Man for others."

That is what we see in Jesus today: He is the Man who lives and dies for others. He is the Man who gives Himself that others may live.

Those whom we recognize as saints today are people who have that mark of Christ upon them: they are men and women who make it their chief purpose in life to give themselves for others. This book indicates that Bill was such a person. A man's man who became God's gentlemen, he allowed God to use him as "a man for others". Thus, he became "a man who made a difference", a difference in us, a difference in the lives of all who knew him.

Why have we told you his story? In part, because we have wanted to honour the memory of a great man. In part also because Bill's story gives reason for all of us to take heart. Today, it is easy to become cynical and to accept the world's claim that for ordinary souls the spiritual life is only a mirage, an unattainable ideal. Bill has proven that that is not so.

At the outset of Bill's story, we wondered where and under what circumstances this little book might be read, wondered about you who are reading these words right now. Whatever your place and whatever your circumstances, we hope that this book with all its testimonies has convinced you of several facts. *For one thing* , we hope that Bill's life has been strong evidence that God does take over a person's life when He is invited to do so: the "Higher Power", by whatever name you know Him, can save and transform your life if you will allow Him to have control. God is not a theory but a Power who changes lives.

Second, we hope that Bill's life has also provided you with strong evidence that St. Paul speaks the truth when he writes that "in everything, God is at work for good with those who love Him", that "we are more than conquerors through Christ who loved us", and that nothing, "neither death nor life, nor anything else in all creation" -- not even the deaths of one's children nor the devastating illness of one's mate nor one's own death through some dread disease -- that "nothing, absolutely nothing, is able to separate us from the love of God which has been revealed in Christ Jesus."

Then, *third*, we hope that Bill's life is also strong evidence to you that true spirituality is not so much concerned with theological arguments and religious doctrines as it is with love, compassion, forgiveness, service to others, freedom from self. To allow God to have control is not to become narrow, judgmental, self-righteous; rather, it is to be made free, to discover that giving is more blessed than receiving and to know that dying to self-centeredness results in being raised to life abundant.

And, *finally*, we hope that Bill's witness has given you strong evidence that, without fuss or fanfare, God can take the talents of an ordinary person, like you, like ourselves, like Bill, and use those talents in ways that may be beyond our imagining. Without God, Bill Crooks would have remained simply a "regular guy", a "man's man", but nothing more. Instead, with God, he was turned into a "man for others", a man who made a difference. Whoever we are, wherever we are, if God is given control, we too can make a difference -- and perhaps a greater difference than we now dream possible.

Our prayer is that that new life which comes alone from God may be both yours and ours as, like Bill, we learn " to walk the Road of Happy Destiny."

about the author:

Hugh MacDonald is a native of Ottawa and a graduate of Carleton and McGill universities. A minister of the United Church of Canada, his last two pastorates were in St. Paul's, Thunder Bay, and Knox-Metropolitan in Regina. In recent years, while continuing in the ministry, he has been professor of the humanities and world religions at Confederation College, Thunder Bay, Canada. He is creator and host of the 24-program educational television series, *Voyage into the Humanities*. Since 1976, he has each summer conducted popular tours to Paris, the Loire Valley, and Provence.

Any reader who wishes to comment on the story of Bill Crooks or who wants to contact Hugh about any matter related to this book is invited to write him directly at 159 Bentwood Drive, Thunder Bay, Ontario, Canada, P7A 7A7. All correspondence will be answered.

* * * * * *

Cover design of this book by *Corporate Graphics Northwest*, Thunder Bay, Ontario, Canada.

Cover inspired by a photograph of Bill Crooks, taken by Angela Meyers, *Jackson Clarion-Ledger*, Jackson, Mississippi, U.S.A.

ISBN 1552124339